*New Design in* WEAVING

*New Design in*
# WEAVING
*Donald J. Willcox*

BRESCIA COLLEGE LIBRARY,
OWENSBORO, KENTUCKY.

VAN NOSTRAND REINHOLD COMPANY
NEW YORK CINCINNATI TORONTO LONDON MELBOURNE

746.1
W697

OTHER BOOKS IN THIS SERIES:

NEW DESIGN IN CERAMICS
NEW DESIGN IN JEWELRY
NEW DESIGN IN STITCHERY
NEW DESIGN IN WOOD

Van Nostrand Reinhold Company Regional Offices:
New York  Cincinnati  Chicago  Millbrae  Dallas

Van Nostrand Reinhold Company International Offices:
London  Toronto  Melbourne

Copyright © 1970 by Litton Educational Publishing, Inc.
Library of Congress Catalog Card Number 70-126868
ISBN 0-442-29466-2

All rights reserved. No part of this work covered by the copyright
hereon may be reproduced or used in any form or by any means—graphic,
electronic, or mechanical, including photocopying, recording, taping,
or information storage and retrieval systems—without written permission
of the publisher. Manufactured in the United States of America

Designed by Myron Hall III
Printed by Halliday Lithograph Corporation
Color printed by Toppan Printing Company, Limited, Japan
Bound by Haddon Bindery

Published by Van Nostrand Reinhold Company
450 West 33rd Street, New York, N.Y. 10001

Published simultaneously in Canada by
Van Nostrand Reinhold, Ltd.

16  15  14  13  12  11  10  9  8  7  6  5  4  3

For
SW, BRL, and KD

# CONTENTS

| | |
|---|---|
| FOREWORD | 8 |
| CONTEMPORARY WEAVING: NEW FRONTIERS | 10 |
|     The Weaver Becomes an Artist | 12 |
|     New Materials in Weaving | 13 |
|     The Loom | 14 |
|     Sculpture: A New Direction | 14 |
| TRADITIONAL WEAVING | 16 |
|     Rya | 16 |
|     Double-Weave | 21 |
|     Damask | 22 |
|     Raanu | 23 |
|     Rosengang | 24 |
|     Rollakan | 25 |
|     Kilim | 26 |
|     Flamskvavnad | 26 |
|     Ikat Dyeing | 27 |
| EXPERIMENTAL WEAVING | 28 |
|     Weaving in Three Dimensions | 28 |
|     Experiments with Metal | 32 |
|     Experiments with Nylon | 33 |
|     Warp Printing | 34 |
|     Adding Objects and Combining Styles | 35 |
| THE PROBLEMS IN SCANDINAVIAN WEAVING | 36 |
|     Techniquism | 37 |
|     Language | 37 |
|     Communication in Weaving | 39 |
|     Functional Weaving | 40 |
| | |
| COLOR PHOTOGRAPHS | 41 |
| RYA | 49 |
| DOUBLE-WEAVE | 58 |
| DAMASK | 65 |
| RAANU | 67 |
| ROSENGANG | 68 |
| ROLLAKAN | 72 |
| FLAMSKVAVNAD | 73 |
| IKAT DYEING | 74 |
| WEAVING WITH A SELF-CONTAINED LOOM | 76 |
| SCULPTURE AND RELIEF | 82 |
| WALL HANGINGS | 93 |
| UNUSUAL MATERIALS | 105 |
| FUNCTIONAL WEAVING | 123 |
| | |
| ACKNOWLEDGMENTS | 126 |
| MATERIALS FOR FURTHER STUDY | 127 |

# FOREWORD

Weaving is a concept. It has many aspects—tradition, technique, styles—but it is before anything else a *concept.* It requires only the interlacing of one strand with another, and therefore the only rule of weaving is that strands must pass over and under each other. *There are no other rules*.

The standard weaving book usually begins with something like: "Weaving is a very old art form," and then continues by serving the reader a slice of history, a sprinkle of theory, and an enormous slab of technical information, including the terminology of weaving, step-by-step instructions in several of the thousands of existing weaving techniques, and page upon page of charts, graphs, and diagrams. This format is almost a stereotype.

But what happens to these books? I have asked this question of hundreds of weavers as I researched this book, and this is the conclusion I reached from the answers I got: some of these books are read and appreciated, others are simply thumbed through; but more often than not the majority are considered like doses of cod liver oil —necessary remedies for specific technical problems.

Weavers complain that few of these books make any attempt to reach the *pulse* of the weaver. They complain, often bitterly, that too many of the books use confusing language, do not distinguish clearly between one technique and another, and describe weaving procedures inaccurately. They say that such books either bore the weaver or frighten off whatever sparks of creativity may have been within him at the time he picked them up. Technical information is addressed to him as if he were a data-processing machine programmed to consume facts. Few of these books really reach out and talk to the weaver, make him think, make him angry, challenge his creativity, stimulate him, give him a real feel for the interlacing of threads.

It is the deliberate intention of the book in hand to *create* controversy. The weaver is a controversial figure, but he is surrounded by a wall of overnourished truisms. Many of these comfortable old truisms have now grown heavy and encrusted with mold. So, in the face of change it is altogether healthy that they be re-examined. This book does that, and it also explores further the potentials within this concept of interlacing strands—this concept of weaving.

The opinions expressed here are the result of a year and a half of research. I have visited over five hundred weavers, mostly Scandinavian, in schools, workshops, galleries, and museums. I have examined their fabrics and their equipment, and I have also sat and talked with them—congenially, over coffee and pastry—about their craft. The result, I think, is not restricted by national borders, but is directed to weavers everywhere and at every level.

The reader under thirty may leap for joy when he runs across one of his own theories offered here, while someone over thirty bleats toward the winds at the same theory. This is altogether to the good because it represents one small success in providing that slice of soul that seems to have been missing from the many books already written on the subject of weaving.

I will initiate the promised controversy by stating—with love and affection—that most weaving has a strong tendency to be boring. This is a challenge, not a criticism: the weaver is competent, tries very hard, and all the rest of the "nice" things that critics say, but, nevertheless, the average weaver is so self-content that he has barely begun to scratch the surface of his abundant medium.

# CONTEMPORARY WEAVING: NEW FRONTIERS

The American poet Lawrence Ferlinghetti once wrote[*]:

             'Truth is not the secret of a few'
                                  yet
you would maybe think so
                    the way some
      librarians
and cultural ambassadors and
              especially museum directors
                                act

This is a barbed jab at those self-appointed intellectuals in every society who surround themselves with a fog of abstractions and who, in the poet's words, "walk around shaking their heads" and spending their energies inventing "high altitude" environments toward which they can point their noses. Such words could have been written for many textile artists, a whole serving of weaving critics, and, unfortunately, many weavers.

For too many years society has dictated weaving styles—told the weaver how to use his creativity and what to create. Indeed, he has long been a slave to his loom rather than its free master, and he has been forced to turn out discreet and completely safe fabrics for so long that he has regarded weaving, until recently, exclusively in those terms. If he were lucky, he might get the opportunity to weave a wall ornament for a nobleman or a narrative tapestry for the clergy. So he channeled all his creative drive into picture-weaving—painting with thread. And he grew weary and reserved about exploring the potentials of his craft.

[*] From Lawrence Ferlinghetti, *A Coney Island of the Mind,* Copyright 1955 by Lawrence Ferlinghetti. Reprinted by permission of New Directions Publishing Corporation.

But now weaving is beginning to grow up. The weaver is stretching his legs—and it's about time! In the past fifteen years he has gradually broken free from the bonds of tradition. He is deliberately defying all the so-called rules on imagery, technique, color, material, even function. This bold new weaver has literally jumped off the wall and is now deep into sculptured form, nontraditional color juxtaposition, and endless combinations of experimental—that is, nontraditional—materials.

Of course, there are still many weavers who shout for the "good old days" and a return to that constructive vocation which produced an endless quantity of towels and table linen. Many of them have been duped into believing the traditional rubbish that weaving is no more than the hand production of fabric with pictures on it. But the climate *is* changing, and the timid weaver, although still conservative in practice, has begun to identify with the younger generation of weavers. Unfortunately, the average critic does a great disservice to all weavers by so often turning his back on change and reserving approval for those works which remain safely within the realm of tradition.

What becomes of this conservative weaver—the one with exceptional ability? Well, he watches what's going on, and when something comes into vogue he begins to dabble with a few ideas of his own—perhaps some shells or pieces of wood on an otherwise conservative work. Of course, he is careful not to stray too far from the paths of safety, because, quite frankly, he's frightened and wonders whether all this experimental imagery is just a passing fancy. This is his first brave step toward acknowledging a freedom that he doesn't understand or know how to use. When will he realize that the shackles are really broken, that he can repossess his loom and make it do anything and everything he wants? This new direction in weaving is indeed no passing fancy—it is here to stay. And it has unlocked the full impact of a handicraft concept that has too long been suppressed.

**THE WEAVER BECOMES AN ARTIST** The direction of contemporary weaving is not surprising if you take just a moment to think about what industrialization has done to the weaver. I think the experience of Finland's Dora Jung, a recognized world leader in damask weaving, is a fair example of why weaving has arrived at its present position. Miss Jung has been around a loom for perhaps forty years. After she finished her schooling, she decided to make weaving her livelihood. At that time, there was a demand for hand-woven damask table linen, curtains, bed linen, and the other household goods traditionally produced by the weaver, so Miss Jung could then earn her living without difficulty. But soon came the Second World War and with it an acute shortage of raw materials. Miss Jung, like countless other weavers, began to weave with paper because paper was the only material available. At the end of the war there was a brief flurry of the old business, but it wasn't long before the weaving mills took over, using improved machinery to mass-produce at a far lower cost what the weaver had formerly made by hand.

Miss Jung was driven out of the household linen business because she was unable to compete with the prices of machine-made goods. To survive, she began to weave fabric fronts for radios, but before long industry invaded that market, too. So finally Dora Jung ended up weaving wall hangings exclusively. She changed from a weaver of functional fabric to a decorator of public buildings and churches—what the Finns now call a "textile artist"—because industry literally *forced* her into it.

Thousands of other weavers around the world have had similar experiences, but, unlike Miss Jung, few of them will admit to such humble beginnings. The contemporary weaver, especially the successful one, has a way of poking his nose into those "high altitudes" described by Ferlinghetti and inflating his image with fancy titles. Let's face it, the weaver mutated into an artist principally because few people could afford his functional ware. If he really wants to claim the title of artist he'll have to abandon his napkin-weaving mentality and begin to think like an artist.

**NEW MATERIALS IN WEAVING** When many of today's established weavers began their careers, wool, linen, and cotton were just about the only materials they used. Now all that has changed: weavers are actively exploring everything from leather to wire. You hear endless conversations on the merits of one material over another—things like "nothing is as good as wool" or "synthetics can never equal natural fibers." I submit that these "high altitude" discussions are utter nonsense. New materials are not there to be judged by traditional standards; they are there to be used for those qualities which make them different. Each one of them has something unique in and of itself: plastic, for example, does not threaten to replace wool, because the potentials of plastic thread are of quite another nature. If the weaver uses new materials for the properties inherent within them, he can never be accused of dishonesty in his woven statements.

Perhaps that is part of the problem. The modern weaver is using materials he doesn't understand. He knows wool, linen, and cotton almost by instinct, but he doesn't understand synthetics like plastic. He may try something with a new material and fail miserably because he has not taken the pains to investigate this new material; or he may want to learn about synthetics, but have no idea where to turn for information. I suggest that the weaver who is interested in working with new materials contact the people who make them—talk to the technicians, chemists, and engineers who perfected them—to find out just what he is working with. He will save himself time and frustration, and in the end he will be applauded for the practical knowledge that he brings to his craft.

**THE LOOM**  For centuries it was assumed that the loom was where weaving began and ended, but many modern weavers are re-examining this notion and challenging its authority. They have found, for example, that the horizontal loom is not equipped to handle certain types of thread, that it does not allow the weaver to view his composition as a whole, nor to make spontaneous changes while he works. Thus weavers are forced to look for other means of supporting their threadwork—such as the self-supporting loom frame and the vertical loom, which had been used by weavers in the past. In addition, they are exploring other techniques, like knotting, crocheting, and knitting, as alternate ways of developing thread form. The conventional loom remains a most useful tool for the weaver, but it is still just a tool, and only one of many ways in which to express the concept of interlacing threads.

**SCULPTURE: A NEW DIRECTION**  A great many modern weavers in Scandinavia have become interested in three-dimensional textiles, and their work has drawn a good deal of bitter criticism from their contemporaries, both weavers and critics. For example, a Finnish designer whose work I greatly admire, and one who is a respected authority on textile design, has attempted to convince me that there is no *raison d'être* for what he labels "experimental weaving," and that much of it, especially sculpture, is an "irresponsible mishandling of expensive material." This argument is sheer snobbery, and what's more it has little logic. If you're going to criticize a modern weaver for using, say, copper tubing instead of wool, then you ought also to scold the Lapps for an old and respected tradition of theirs—tin-thread embroidery.

Ferlinghetti said that this type of intellectualism made him feel "constipated." Certainly a race of men that has reached the moon is far too advanced to be narrow-minded about art forms. Perhaps the conservative weaver has reason to be timid—his creative drive has been stifled for so long. But he should try to be optimistic. Experimental weaving is stirring up long dormant but healthy forces. And what the weaver is witnessing now is just the beginning of a dynamic thrust forward.

Contemporary weaving has opened the door to broad exploration. Young eyes are comparing modern and traditional pieces and often finding the latter bland and uninteresting. This book contains many examples of weaving, a number of them traditional Scandinavian pieces that use only natural materials or one type of yarn throughout. In addition, however, there are works by a delightful young generation of weavers who have turned their backs on "the rules" and tried just about every combination imaginable. These illustrations should convince you as no words ever could that the old rules of weaving are no longer relevant. The weaver is free to use anything he needs to make his statement and to carry it to its furthest point.

## TRADITIONAL WEAVING

Here and in the section that follows, I will discuss traditional and experimental weaving techniques. Some confusion exists about the names commonly given to traditional Scandinavian techniques, depending on whether you are discussing Sweden, Denmark, Norway, or Finland, and I will go into this in more detail further on. For now let me say just that it is unimportant—names are simply a convenient method for identification. What *is* important is the concept behind the name. I have elected to approach each technique from this standpoint—in other words, what the weaver can hope to gain from a technique, what kind of imagery it produces, and what its possibilities are in contemporary design. If the reader desires further information, he can refer to Materials for Further Study in the back of the book, where I have listed Scandinavian weaving books that provide step-by-step weaving instructions in English, as well as supply sources for weaving materials. It is hoped that this book will open more doors for the weaver—introduce him to techniques that may be unfamiliar and stimulate him to explore further those he feels he can use to his own personal advantage.

**RYA** Contrary to popular belief, the term *rya* describes a knotting technique and not a rug. The word, which is believed to come from Sweden, means "rough" and refers to the deep pile, shag, or nap produced by knotting bunches of yarn to warp threads. In Finland, where the technique is most highly advanced, it is called *ryijy,* pronounced róo-ee-you.

Scandinavian use of the rya technique dates back to the thirteenth century and perhaps earlier. Then ryas were used principally as protection against the cold, and the pile was often produced on both sides to provide greater warmth. For all practical purposes, the rya shag was a man-made substitute for animal fur. Until the first part of the nineteenth century ryas were used for bed covers by Swedish soldiers and sailors, and in Norway it was not uncommon to find them shielding fishermen in open boats. The versatile rya was also used as a sleigh cover, as a doorway curtain for insulation, as a colorful wall decoration, as barter for food and medicine and farm supplies, and even as payment for taxes and overdue accounts.

Woven ryas were precious possessions in every family, often the most coveted part of a bride's dowry. In fact, records indicate that many young Scandinavian girls were married while kneeling on the almost sacred family rya. The rya was rarely if ever used as a floor covering because it was, and still is, too highly valued among Scandinavians to fall victim to dirty snow- and mud-spattered boots. It is the American tourist in Scandinavia who has redefined the rya as rug, and it has taken the American dollar to pull it off the bed or wall and put it on the floor.

Rya yarn was formerly dyed with colors extracted from plants and trees—birch bark, leaves, camomile, wild rosemary, spruce cones, and alder barks were some sources. Early ryas were mostly pictorial, depicting trees, flowers, birds, and especially religious symbols. In the twentieth century, however, colors and designs became much freer. Two modern designs in rya weaving which are probably familiar to most readers are the patterns of exploding color and the ones with subtle gradations of tone.

Early ryas varied in size and weight, some weighing as much as 40 pounds (they contained anywhere from 66 to 304 knots per square decimeter). Looms were so narrow in the old days that ryas were often woven in halves and then seamed together down the center. The modern rya is usually about 4½ by 6 feet in size, although this, too, varies. Today, looms are available in broader widths for rya weaving, and there are now even machines that can tie rya knots mechanically.

To begin a rya, the weaver dresses the loom warp in the usual manner. He then knots clumps, or bunches, of yarn onto these warp threads to create the pile. Traditionally these bunches would contain from two to six separate strands (depending on the thickness and denseness of the pile). The strands, which range from 3½ to 6 inches in length, are arranged within each clump by color, and the clumps are knotted around pairs of warp threads. After the clumps have been knotted the full width of the warp, the weaver beats in from six to ten rows of weft, or filler, yarn and then repeats the knotting procedure again. Traditionalists insist that all knot ends be trimmed exactly even. In old ryas the pile varied from ½ to ¾ inches long; in contemporary ryas it varies from 1¼ to 3 inches. In Figure 13, there are detailed diagrams illustrating a variety of knotting techniques for the rya. As indicated, knot *g* is the most commonly used in modern rya weaving. Most rya weavers work from a full-sized cartoon, usually a watercolor. The cartoon is normally made in sections, anywhere from 12 to 18 inches per section, and tacked onto the loom under the warp. Most modern rya weavers work by themselves, but in Finland weavers occasionally knot in pairs, one at each end of the bench working across the warp from the outside toward the center. This, of course, speeds up the knotting process considerably. A modern rya of standard size will contain approximately twenty thousand hand-knotted tufts and will take an experienced weaver from two and one-half to three and one-half weeks to complete. Now you can understand why the rya is such a prized possession and why the Scandinavian doesn't usually walk on it!

There are a number of theories on how to estimate the amount of yarn needed for a rya. I've found them all confusing except one: simply work up a pattern or cartoon and then weave a miniature rya of about 12 by 16 inches in that exact pattern. If you keep a record of how much yarn you use in each color and then multiply that amount by the number of times your sample will fit into your full-sized pattern, you will have a close approximation of the quantity to buy.

As you can see, tradition keeps a tight, almost iron grip on the weaving of ryas. Accordingly, the rya is supposed to be made only from wool, always rectangular in shape, and always hung vertically. These rules are time-honored nonsense, and it is now time to break them in order to discover the endless potentials of the rya technique. The Finns, who often try to claim ownership of the technique, are the most conservative in using it. In January, 1969, for example, the Bayer Chemical Company held an exhibition at the design center in Helsinki to introduce a synthetic rya yarn called Dralon to Finnish weavers. Dralon was reputed to have advantages over wool—it was colorfast, lighter in weight, nonallergenic, resistant to stain, mothproof, and strong—all of which made it more suitable for the rya floor coverings the company produced. Although the exhibition was received with interest by the general public, the attitude of the press and of Finnish weavers was that "a rya isn't a rya unless it's made out of wool," and many of the well-meaning weavers who had designed ryas for Bayer were attacked for "selling out." So you see, the rya is not something to be tampered with in Finland—it is as sacred to the Finns as the flag and sauna.

Outside of Finland, however, Scandinavians are experimenting endlessly with the technique, and they have discovered that it offers unlimited potential for nontraditional imagery. The rya has a "living quality" that is very much in harmony with modern design: its colors will intensify and its surface will change according to the way the light hits it or the way its deep pile is brushed. Then, too, it is eminently suited to works in high relief. For example, the number of strands within each clump can be varied; strands can be trimmed at different lengths, from very short to, say, 10 or 12 inches; shag ends can be braided, tied with wooden beads, left uncut, or knotted; and several clumps can be tied into long pigtails down the front of the rya. Other possibilities include knotting with more than one material, perhaps wool and plastic; or using rya knots in a collage with plain weaving, embroidery, or some other interesting surface. In addition, commercial rya yarn is ideal for use in other needlecrafts, particularly crocheting. And, of course, rya shag can be used for trim on collars, cuffs, and hems; for wearing apparel such as sweaters, shawls, hats, coats, dresses, and handbags; and for furniture coverings and dozens of other useful items for the home.

A word about the "rya kit," a mutation of the rya technique produced especially for export from Scandinavia. Before you shudder at the idea, I should tell you that although it does little to stimulate original design, it does give the bashful weaver that initial push he may need to try something like rya on his own, and it is a good way for the beginner to get the feel of rya knotting. The patterns have been designed by well-qualified weavers, many of them educators. The rya kit comes complete with synthetic backing, needles, yarn, pattern, and directions. It does not require the use of a loom—shag clumps are simply knotted onto the backing in accordance with the pattern. These rya kits should never be taken as an end in themselves; they are learning tools to develop a feeling for the knot and the potentials of shag. Once they have served that purpose, they should be abandoned in favor of expressing the rya technique freely and in a personal way.

**DOUBLE-WEAVE**  In Finland this technique is called *takana,* but elsewhere in Scandinavia it is known as double-weave or *finnvav.* Traditionally, and here again the Finns are the most tradition-bound, double-weave calls for a linen warp and weft; but tradition aside, it can be used with any combination of materials, including a full range of synthetic and metal fibers.

The purpose of the technique is twofold: on the one hand, it produces a fabric that has a finished, or front, surface on both sides; on the other hand, it allows the weaver to develop patterns with definite, hard-edge color imagery. The technique is also excellent for studies in transparency because of its two finished surfaces. For example, patterns can be built on front and back surfaces to harmonize or complement each other when the light strikes them. Similarly, the illusion of depth can be created on an otherwise flat-surfaced fabric.

Still another use of the technique is building relief, such as was done by Danish weaver Nana Nissen in Figure 19. Miss Nissen draped a long woven fabric over a dowel and then seamed the two ends together in a continuous piece so that the finished underside of the fabric is clearly visible through the large open space in the front. As you can see, she has appliquéd beads on the back surface to heighten the contrast, but even without these beads the juxtaposition of open space and woven fabric would still be striking.

In Figure 23 Danish weaver Kirsten Dehlholm has woven double-weave with transparent plastic in three colors—the same type of plastic used in making bags. The piece is designed so that light will illuminate its internal structure, and Miss Dehlholm has added dimension to the composition by joining the surfaces at intervals to create pockets. These pockets bulge with various bits of scrap material, including onion skin, ink-stained tissue, and even leaves, thus giving even more fullness to the relief.

Double-weave is not easy to set up on the loom: the pattern must be carefully planned in advance. Briefly, the heddles are tied so that the warp is divided approximately in half, with each separate half then divided in half a second time. Two sheds are worked at once, and the two front surfaces are woven into one thickness at the same time.

**DAMASK**   Traditionally, damask is woven with a linen warp and weft to produce a firm, reversible fabric. The technique requires the use of a draw loom especially constructed to raise not only groups of warp threads, but individual warp threads as well. A draw loom has a wooden frame that projects out over the weaver's bench and holds the equivalent of a second set of harnesses that work individual warp threads independently of the loom heddles. This allows the weaver to produce distinct warp or weft patterns and also to weave monochromatic designs like white on white. It is also possible to do studies in transparency and hard-edge imagery with the damask technique.

At the beginning of the twentieth century, damask weaving was still very popular among hand-weavers in Scandinavia, but today most damask is done industrially, and up until recently it was next to impossible to purchase a draw loom, even in Scandinavia. Another reason why there are so few damask weavers around today is that the technique is one of the most complicated and time-consuming in weaving. The Ateneum, Finland's national design school, is still teaching damask, even though student interest is failing. Finland's Dora Jung and her associates, however, continue to produce some of the most inventive damask weaving in the modern world. Miss Jung begins her patterns from small drawings and then enlarges them into full-sized cartoons. The cartoon is cut into pieces horizontally, and each piece is tacked to the loom directly under the warp as that section is woven. Examples of Miss Jung's work are featured in Figures 37 through 43.

**RAANU** Although some authorities may disagree with me on this point, I consider raanu to be more a specific type of pattern than a separate technique. A raanu is a thick, coarsely woven cover, much like a rug, traditionally made by the Scandinavian Lapp. The distinguishing characteristic of the Lapp raanu is its pattern of horizontal stripes, frequently in brilliant colors (see Figure 44). Quite often these colors were arranged to tell a story about nature, and the presence or absence of color seems to have been somewhat regional among the Lapps. The Finns, for example, used color prolifically, whereas some of the Norwegian Lapps wove their raanu in striped tones of black, white, and gray.

Early Lapp weavers were likely to use old rags or discarded clothing cut into strips for their raanu, but a modern raanu weaver like Elsa Montell-Saanio from the tiny Arctic village of Oikaraien in Finland uses wool for her work. Otherwise, Mrs. Saanio retains a maximum of tradition in her designs. Some of her dyes are extracted from regional plant life: she uses birch leaves boiled in water to develop her yellows and the Suopursu flower that grows on the moors to produce her golds. To these plant-derived colors she adds commercial oxides to prevent running and fading.

Another distinguishing mark of the raanu is its braid. In the old raanu, braids appeared at the top and bottom and often along the sides, at intervals of 10 to 12 inches. These were both decorative and functional: their most important use was in tieing raanu together to form the *kota,* the traditional teepee dwelling of the Lapp (see Figure 46). Mrs. Saanio believes that the top braid was also used to tie the warp to a vertical loom, the type used by early Lapps to produce their raanu.

In addition to its function in portable-home building, the raanu served many other purposes. The early Lapp migrated frequently, and he used the raanu as a body cover in the frigid Arctic climate. He also used it to cover his sleigh and often as a sail on his boat.

A modern raanu is woven on a horizontal loom with two kinds of thread: distaff for the warp and a thick, loosely spun yarn for the weft. This combination produces a texture that is thick and soft, like felt. The raanu stripe has also been adopted by several Finnish weavers for scarves and shawls. These articles are usually woven with a loose, soft yarn called Topsy, and finished off with braid or small, hand-dyed wooden beads.

For additional information on Lapp weaving, one excellent reference source is *The People of Eight Seasons* by Ernst Manker.

**ROSENGANG** The rosengang or rose-path technique is a weft-faced weave derived from twill and characterized by a weft that floats, or flows out over the warp in a pattern that resembles a series of roses. Traditional rosengang calls for a tabby ground in which two picks are followed by a pattern pick that floats out loosely across the front surface, but in reverse, or bound, rosengang the weft lies loosely on the reverse side of the fabric and does not form the pattern. Four treadles at different floats are normally used to weave rosengang.

Contemporary use of the technique affords a type of woven calligraphy similar to Japanese lettering, especially when hand-drawn picks are run out freely across the warp. Even bolder designs can be achieved by alternating yarn thickness, types of yarn, and particularly yarn colors. Helen Barynina, formerly of Sweden and now in Montreal, uses the technique to develop a surface topography of brushlike strokes that are rhythmic, rippling, and almost musical. Her work is illustrated in Figures 48 and 50.

**ROLLAKAN** Rollakan is one of several weft reps with an interlocked weave. Weft threads are picked in by hand with a butterfly bobbin (yarn wrapped around the hand) along a straight line in the horizontal warp. Rep areas are interlocked, also by hand, either at each inlay or at alternate inlays. Slits caused by changing the color of the weft are double-locked on the reverse side, which faces the weaver while he is at the loom.

Rollakan produces geometric blocks of pattern, the smallest unit generally a square comprising two, four, six, or eight warp threads and as many weft threads as are required to complete it. One use of rollakan is illustrated in Figure 57, where blocks of various sizes and colors are developed into an overall geometric pattern. Pictorial imagery of the sort in Figure 59 is produced with smaller blocks of the same color in zigzag lines. Rollakan produces a much smoother surface than other interlocked weaves and is therefore not the best technique for surface relief. However, interesting surface contrasts can be developed by using yarns of varying thickness and color, or of different types.

The technique was often used for seat cushions, and the name rollakan is a corruption of the Swedish word *ryglakan,* which refers to the wall at the back of a seat. Variations include Scanian rollakan, diagonal rollakan, zigzag rollakan, and Norwegian rollakan. An excellent source for further information on rollakan weaving is the *Manual of Swedish Handweaving* by Ulla Cyrus.

**KILIM** Like rollakan, the pattern in kilim is picked in by hand with a butterfly bobbin—but unlike rollakan, yarns of different color are laid in without being interlocked. This produces open slits in the fabric, and the movement in weaving is constantly toward the sides to hold the fabric together. The pattern of kilim is geometric, but it is much more sculptural than rollakan because of its slits, which, if exaggerated, can produce very bold relief. Kilim is reversible and can be used with rollakan and many other techniques. It is also adaptable for use with yarns of varying thicknesses and types.

**FLAMSKVAVNAD** A technique highly developed in Sweden, flamskvavnad is also referred to as high-warp tapestry or Flemish weaving. Traditionally it is woven on a linen warp stretched vertically on a vertical loom. The warp threads are laid in exact order, so many to the inch according to the desired texture of the work, by means of a laced cord at the top of the warp. The weft is usually wool, and each color is wound onto a separate tapestry bobbin that is pointed at one end. A round stick is used for the shed; it is inserted between alternate warp threads and kept suspended. Normally, a full-sized color cartoon is attached to the loom behind the warp in flamskvavnand. Weaving is begun at the bottom, and the pattern is woven piece by piece, color by color. The separate sections are then connected by toothing, with the weft from the adjacent color areas alternately crossing the same warp thread. Warp lines that are double or single weft-locked are comparatively rare in this type of weaving.

One of the beauties of flamskvavnad is that with the vertical loom the weaver has the whole composition in front of him all the time he is working, and not the usual fragmented parts. In contemporary weaving, the flamskvavnad technique is often combined with other styles, particularly rya.

**IKAT DYEING** This is actually not a weaving technique, but a process for dyeing yarn. Ikat dyeing probably originated in India and then spread to Scandinavia, where it was used extensively in Finland and parts of Sweden during the late eighteenth century. Today it has become a popular method for coloring yarn among young weavers all over Scandinavia.

An essential tool for ikat dyeing is the ikat stick (see Figures 64 and 65), which is actually nothing more than a pine stick about 2 inches square and 3 to 4 feet long, with dowels at the top and bottom. Warp yarn is wound around the dowels and then tied or bound at intervals with thin yarn, according to the pattern desired. (Notches cut into the stick indicate points at which the yarn is to be tied.) The stick is dunked into a long, narrow trough of dye, one side at a time. The parts of the yarn that are tied will not absorb dye if they are bound tightly, so they must be secured to prevent any leakage. For multicolored effects, for each color the sections to be dyed are exposed, and the rest is tied off. After the yarn is dry, it is set on the loom in the usual manner.

Colored portions on ikat-dyed yarn have feathery rather than even edges, and the yarn is often woven into geometric patterns like the ones in Figures 66 through 68. For a streaked or patchy effect, the yarn can be knotted instead of tied, and the knots dipped in dye. Hand-dyeing the warp yarns (either singly or in bunches) with a dauber will produce subtle gradations of tone. This can be done by simply stretching warp yarns for dyeing on a long table.

Two contemporary weavers, Grete Balle of Denmark and Siri Blackstad of Norway, have experimented with yarn dyed in luminous paint that glows in the dark. Miss Blackstad has used English yarn, predyed for making theater costumes, and Miss Balle has done high relief with Day-Glo-painted yarn woven into a black, shadow-box frame. When the box is illuminated, the results are startling: threads come to life, magnified, and the onlooker gets something like a microscopic view of the internal structure of the weaving. Other contemporary weavers who deserve mention for their experiments with ikat dyeing include students at the Goteborg Konstindustriskolan, and the Danish weaver Annette Jersild.

## EXPERIMENTAL WEAVING

**WEAVING IN THREE DIMENSIONS**  There are still a number of weavers who respond with surprise to three-dimensional weaving and who still consider it something new, something of a fad or a style. It is none of these things, however, and it is as consistent with the concept of interlacing strands as is the use of thread. There is no such thing as two-dimensional thread: every single thread, no matter how fine it is, has circumference and surface texture, and every single thread is itself a separate, three-dimensional form. When threads are run over and under each other, the results will also be three dimensional. In other words, every piece of weaving is actually a study in relief, a study which by its very composition contains the elements of sculpture.

The modern weaver who attempts sculpture must be admired for breaking with a tradition that has kept him shackled to his loom. Nevertheless, he is caught in a dilemma: he has put on a hat that doesn't quite fit his head. For example, he may think that woven relief is something that sticks out from the wall, and so he sews something like a shell onto a wall hanging and then calls it a sculptured surface. It is clear that he doesn't know the first thing about the problems and potentials of dimension. And it is equally clear that although he chooses to call himself "sculptor," he is still thinking along the lines of flat-surface fabric.

The weaver shouldn't be blamed for his ignorance; he hasn't been trained to be a sculptor. With the proper schooling, and once he puts his mind to it, the modern weaver will undoubtedly wear the sculptor's hat with ease. Education is the place to begin, and fortunately for the young weaver many textile schools are now offering courses for weavers in three-dimensional design concepts.

Relief is not woven like a table napkin. Yarn must be approached differently—as an object that has mass and texture *independent* of the surface into which it is woven. You can't just add bits and pieces to a piece of weaving, or stuff it and prop it to give it bulk, and then think that you have created sculpture. All the elements of your composition—color, texture, and individual shapes—must relate to one another and contribute to the total form. And weaving that is not supported by a wall—free-standing or free-hanging form—must be disciplined in terms of its own mass and also in terms of the space that it invades: the immediate, or *negative,* space that silhouettes it, the wall behind it, and the room it occupies.

One way to begin exploring the problems of free-standing sculpture is to lift the wall hanging off the wall and simply let it drop freely onto the floor. Chances are it will land in a heap—a form that is admittedly undisciplined, yet is already self-supporting. Now try starch, a stiffening agent, some wire, brass thread, copper tubing, or just a coat hanger for structural support. With these additions you have already begun to give definition to your undisciplined heap.

As a second step you can try a self-contained loom to support your form. This is a loom frame used in the actual weaving and then retained as part of the finished form. The idea is to design the loom as a skeleton for your sculpture and then to weave within it and around it as you choose. Examples of this type of three-dimensional weaving are the mobiles of Nana Nissen illustrated in Figures 69 and 70. Miss Nissen wired sticks of bamboo together to form polyhedrons and then created several woven surfaces in wool within those frameworks. In this type of work any number of materials are suitable for making the loom, among them wood, wire, tubing, and plastic, as well as natural forms such as U-shaped tree limbs.

Rope knotting is an age-old skill that has gone practically unnoticed among modern weavers, and one that has unlimited potential for sculpture in weaving. During a visit to the Royal Danish Navy Yard at Holmen near Copenhagen, I watched five elderly men weaving and knotting solid sculptural forms which were to be used as bumpers to prevent ships from rubbing against their moorings. These five men, former sailors, are all that remains of a once-active rope-knotting yard, and they have spent most of their lives doing this kind of work. They explained to me that the Royal Navy has converted from hemp and jute to nylon for their bumpers, and since nylon doesn't wear out, the yard is soon to be abandoned. With little to do now, the five occupy their time by weaving and knotting animal forms. I asked them if any weavers had come to visit them recently, and they told they hadn't had any visitors for years. Weavers, in Copenhagen right now dozens upon dozens of your fellow craftsmen are trying to figure out how to do exactly what these old sailors are doing —support weaving without a wall! And unless someone among you at least takes the trouble to investigate the possibilities of knotting, these skills will pass from sight and be forgotten in a few years.

Grete Balle has been experimenting with ways to develop rigid forms on wall hangings. In her bold relief entitled "Dark Foggy Figure" (Figure 84), she laid woven fabric over a lamp shade and coated the part just over the shade with glue. After the glue hardened, she was able to remove the lamp shade and the glue-stiffened fabric stood by itself. In Figure 87, Kirsten Dehlholm has attempted still another kind of sculptured relief. The piece measures about 6 by 13 feet and is made out of sisal, string, fish line, and tow. The mushroom forms that seem to grow out of the background were developed by splicing loose loops in the weft with bast, celluloid, and wire. Some of the bound loops were left as is and others were cut at the top, bound to within 2 inches of the end, and then brushed open to form mushroom caps. To heighten the organic effect, this weaving is suspended from the ceiling over a tree branch so that it touches the floor on one side and runs out along the floor on the other.

Still another possibility for wall reliefs is to knit or crochet forms on a flat, woven fabric and then stuff the forms or leave them limp. Anything from stocking-caps to imaginative abstractions can be used. Harmonious effects are best achieved in this type of form building when yarns of the same type are used for both weaving and needlework. Then the forms do not come across as an afterthought, but blend as part of the whole.

**EXPERIMENTS WITH METAL** I've seen a number of interesting works by Scandinavian weavers using metal, including pieces out of soft steel, copper, brass, silver, and even coat hangers. Wire seems to work well enough in the weft, or in the warp and weft on a vertical loom, but weavers who have attempted to use wire for the warp on a horizontal loom have encountered problems with tension and have found it ruinous to their hands.

The work of Danish weaver Puk Lippmann, featured in Figures 143 and 144, is made out of various kinds of yarn and copper tubing. As preparation for her work, Miss Lippmann learned how to solder copper. She then built herself an enormous S-shaped copper frame that would support maximum internal tension and proceeded to weave yarn and more copper tubing in various open-work patterns within the frame. The result is appropriately called "Space Screen," and it is beautiful to look at and functions perfectly as a room divider. In answer to critics who rebuked her for using more than one material in her weaving, Miss Lippmann now intends to weave the same piece solely of soldered tubing. In addition, she has been invited by a Swedish factory producing stainless steel to weave for them a labyrinth of welded steel tubing that is not only free-standing, but is an environment to actually be entered.

In Figure 141, Birgitta Mellentin has knotted a room divider on a vertical wooden frame, using brass tubing and yarns in yellow and gold tones that blend with the metal. Clara Salander, whose work is shown in Figure 139, has created a sculptured form of sheet brass and then used the open space in the center as a loom for strands of nylon and glass beads. Although the brass here is used flat, it could as well have been hammered or bent into full, three-dimensional form.

**EXPERIMENTS WITH NYLON**  A number of Scandinavian weavers have been attracted to nylon for weaving, not only because it is translucent, but because it is available in such a variety of thicknesses. The exceptional girth of some of this nylon seems to challenge the weaver into making bold, larger-than-life statements with thread. For example, I've seen wall hangings using nylon weft measuring 2½ inches in diameter—the same type of rope used to moor trans-Atlantic steamers!

There are, however, a number of technical problems involved in the use of nylon. For one thing, it seems to have many of the drawbacks of the old-fashioned girdle. It's forever moving around, slipping, unraveling, and coming untied—all of which upsets the tension in a piece of weaving. What inevitably happens is that when the weaver develops a fine piece of nylon weaving on the loom—one with open spaces that really please him—the moment he removes it from the loom, the nylon begins to shrivel, closing up the spaces and altering the pattern. Bodil Bodtker-Naess has tried to remedy this situation by stretching her finished weaving (she uses nylon for both warp and weft) between a frame of aluminum (see Figures 150 and 151). With this method, she retains some but not all of the tension that was present when the piece was still on the loom. Mrs. Bodtker-Naess also finds it essential to bind warp ends around her stretcher with natural fiber to keep the nylon from untying.

As if all that weren't enough, Mrs. Bodtker-Naess reports that lighter-colored nylon, especially white, seems to yellow with age. She compensates for this color change by planning for it ahead of time in her color scheme. Everything considered, however, it seems that nylon is not the most ideal material to use by itself for weaving. It is probably most successful when combined with other materials in the weft to provide sharp contrasts in texture.

**WARP PRINTING** This is an experimental coloring process using regular pigment dyes and a silk screen. It is being done mainly by English weavers, but a number of students at the Goteborg Konstindustriskolan are also trying it out. The work I've seen has been restricted to cotton and linen warps, because a smooth or an untextured surface is advisable for printing in this manner.

Color areas in a warp-printed fabric overlap and blend impressionistically, and thus the weaver can develop striking pattern imagery without resorting to complicated loom techniques. Warp printing is also excellent for studies in transparency. For instance, the weaver can print with one color on the warp and then weave a weft of another color across the already existing print.

Warp printing can be done on or off the loom, but Goteborg students report that the simplest way is to print the warp while it is on the loom. This will limit the size of the print to the area between the front beam and the harnesses, but it also eliminates the problems of tension loss and pattern change, both of which occur when printing off the loom is not done with care.

To print on the loom, first the warp is stretched tight and then a backing board or print plate (Goteborg students used one made out of wood and covered with felt) is placed under the threads. The silk screen goes on top of the warp threads, and the dye is run across the screen with a scraper. The dye pigment must be completely dry before the warp is wound.

To print off the loom, the warp is set on the loom as usual, and then a few weft threads are thrown in at intervals of about every 1½ feet to keep the warp tied in place. The warp is removed from the loom, along with the beams and harness, placed on a long table, and printed with a silk screen. Then it is returned to the loom, together with beams and harness. As a final step, the temporary weft threads are removed. Printing in this manner allows for much larger imagery.

A variation of warp printing involves the silk-screening of fabric after it has been woven and removed from the loom. This method is simpler, but not as interesting as warp printing, and it does not allow for as much experiment with transparency. A plain weave or one with only a single-color thread should be used.

**ADDING OBJECTS AND COMBINING STYLES**  To develop interesting surface contrasts, weaving can also be combined with other thread techniques and with decorative objects, objects found in nature, or industrial fragments. I call your attention to the illustrations in the picture section of this book, which include a number of fascinating examples of weaving with appliqué, with embroidery knots, crochet, and with pulled-thread embroidery.

# THE PROBLEMS IN SCANDINAVIAN WEAVING

When I began to write this book, I had to choose between either singing the praises of Scandinavian weaving or really exposing its pulse. I have tried to follow the latter path, and I hope I have grappled with some of the problems the weaver faces every day during the quiet hours when he is at his loom.

Scandinavia is undoubtedly a fertile area for the contemporary weaver, but it still is a place where the weaver is overwhelmed by tradition and inhibited by too much technical competence. The ability to weave well has too often become a substitute for the ability to weave *creatively.* And the weaver's vision as an artist has become so clouded by images from the past that he cannot see the wealth of explorative freedom just beyond his fingertips.

Fewer than half-a-dozen of the thousands of weavers in Norway, for example, have used nontraditional materials in their work or attempted disciplined three-dimensional design. The situation in Finland is a little happier, but styles are still strongly guided by "high altitude" critics; and Sweden's abundant weaving talent is tightly controlled by the old guard of "constipated intellectuals." Even in Denmark, known to be the most experimental and the least traditional of the Scandinavian countries, it is still almost impossible to sell experimental work. Danes have grown so conscious of design aesthetics that they are unable to equate textile with art—textile being a lower form of endeavor than, for example, chair. Denmark is also a poor place to hold a weaving exhibition. At the two major exhibitions in Copenhagen each year, Den Fri and Charlottenborg, all the handicrafts including weaving, ceramics, embroidery, and glass are lumped together in a dreary corner to distinguish them from the "fine arts" of sculpture and painting. But why should the Danish weaver who submits a fine example of sculptured relief be exhibited with tea cozies? And why should all these displays of weaving be reviewed only on the woman's page, along with the recipes, instead of with the fine arts where they belong?

**TECHNIQUISM**  There is much too much emphasis on learning techniques for their own sake in Scandinavia, and not enough emphasis on really learning how to use them. Ateneum students in Finland, for instance, have long been required to master a complicated technique like damask because it is a time-honored tradition, even though it has been virtually impossible to buy a new damask loom until very recently. I'm not underrating knowledge—that's fine—I'm just pointing out that this kind of thing has been carried to an extreme and has caused a loss of perspective among weavers. The young especially are stifled by this system, and experimentation in new areas is severely retarded.

Fortunately, three-dimensional form has provided a breather from some of this techniquism. In traditional weaving, the woven surface is like a theater in which to display the technical virtuosity of the weaver. But in relief, all that is relegated to the sidelines—the woven surface is just one of several elements in the composition. So some weavers, at least, are able to see again the woven surface in terms of its texture, its colors, and its contours.

**LANGUAGE**  Another trouble area in weaving is terminology. There are thousands of ways to interlace thread, and each of these has been given a name by a writer, a critic, or a weaver. Now all these people who have created this immense weaving vocabulary can't agree on definitions. Gobelin, for example, can mean wall hanging, or a specific technique, or picture-weaving in general. The same is true for terms like flamskvavnad and tapestry. And to make matters worse, each country will hang its own label on a technique. Flamskvavnad to a Norwegian is Flemish weaving to a Swiss, and each is sure that his technique is different from the other, when in fact they are the same. There are even regional differences in terminology within a single country! So now everyone is scratching his head and wondering what to call what! It's too bad that the weaver so often feels compelled to define instead of to *understand* what he's doing. It simply makes him a slave to technique when he should be its master. And the poor student is at first frightened by all this name-calling and then lapses into utter boredom. Of course, the final bitter pill comes later, when this young weaver ventures into untried areas. Some overzealous critic comes along and dubs his work "free rosengang" or "art-form Gobelin." The confusion grows denser.

Another case of high-altitude intellectualism among weavers—and this time I'm scolding mostly the critic—is their fondness for labeling look-alikes. We've all heard or read somewhere that A weaves like B, or that C's work is definitely Swedish-looking or Finnish-looking or—and this is the *coup de grâce*—primitive-looking!

These comparisons are ridiculous, and what's more they're malicious, because they imply that the weaver in question has no talent and is simply copying someone else's style. Of course weavers are influenced by one another—all artists are. And no one nationality has exclusive rights to a given technique. After all, the Finns are generally credited with inventing the rya, but the rya historian at the National Museum of Finland tells me that the Finns got it from the Swedes.

And only God knows where the Swedes got it.

There's a Norwegian Lapp woman in a tiny Arctic village who weaves three-dimensional forms with tar yarn and sisal. You may immediately assume that she's copying the work of some well-known contemporary weaver, but when you ask her she tells you that she's been inspired to weave the way she does by the nets, hanging up to dry along the beach, that she can see from her window, and that she uses the same material in her work as does the local fisherman.

So you see, nobody owns imagery: there are similarities in all environments, no matter how they differ. The next time you hear someone shout look-alike over a composition with familiar elements, challenge him to find a composition that is completely unique.

**COMMUNICATION IN WEAVING** Despite all this fondness for labels and look-alikes, Scandinavian weavers actually have a difficult time exchanging ideas with one another—perhaps because they feel rivalry rather than kinship for their fellow weavers. Craft organizations do exist where the weaver can go and meet with other weavers, but these are usually cliquish and conservative—qualities which scare off the young and the experimenter. Exhibitions from one country to another are generally influenced by conservative opinions, and if the show is not "safe," it never gets off the ground. If weavers could just organize themselves the way other people in the arts do, hold symposiums and meet with artists from other fields, they would encourage and stimulate individual weavers and they would also advance the cause of weaving immeasurably. And if the young weaver would stop hiding and speak out against all this conservatism and traditionalism, he, too, could bring about healthy change.

**FUNCTIONAL WEAVING**   It's ironic, but with all the wall hangings and sculpture being done, the modern weaver seems to have forgotten his origins as a weaver of household goods. I visited every weaving school in Scandinavia, and I found only a half-dozen students who had ever tried their skill at something other than a wall hanging. Does this mean that the weaver thinks that a wall hanging is the only proper outlet for his abundant energies? Or perhaps he feels that weaving useful items is beneath his dignity as a "textile artist"? I submit that he can use all his talents and creative freedom to weave scarves, curtains, neckties, handbags, sweaters, ponchos, and dresses. In fact, he has the opportunity to become a dynamic force within the fashion world, and he can also provide the public with more beauty in the articles they use every day.

These have all been very real problems in weaving today, but the picture is still far from bleak. I could cite countless instances of professional societies that have helped the weaver—to develop sales outlets, to obtain raw material, and to spread the gospel of weaving in general. I could build a very strong case for the Scandinavian man-on-the-street, who uses the product of the weaver in his home, in his office, and in his public buildings. And I could also tell you of so many farm wives who supplement their husbands' incomes by weaving and who still grow their own flax for linen or raise their own sheep for wool. Indeed, there is no lack of weaving talent in Scandinavia, nor is there a lack of knowledge about it or respect and love for the weaver's craft. But the concept of weaving creatively is still in its infancy, and therein lies a wealth of new opportunity for personal expression.

C-1. Detail of wool tapestry by Synnove Aurdal of Norway. (Courtesy of *Bonytt* magazine.)

C-1

C-2. "Missa Monserata," rya in wool, 4½ by 6 feet. By Oili Maki of Finland.

C-3. "Noidanketta," transparency in linen by Maija Kolsi-Makela of Finland. (Courtesy of Helmi Vuorelma.)

C-4. "Purple Sea" in wool. By Oili Maki of Finland.

C-2

C-3

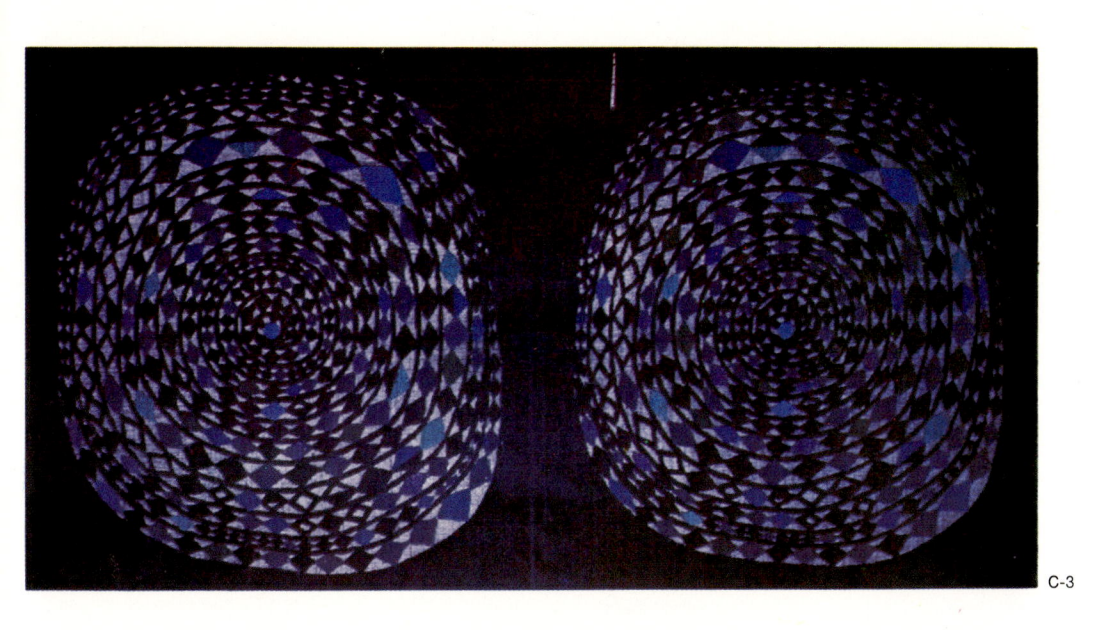

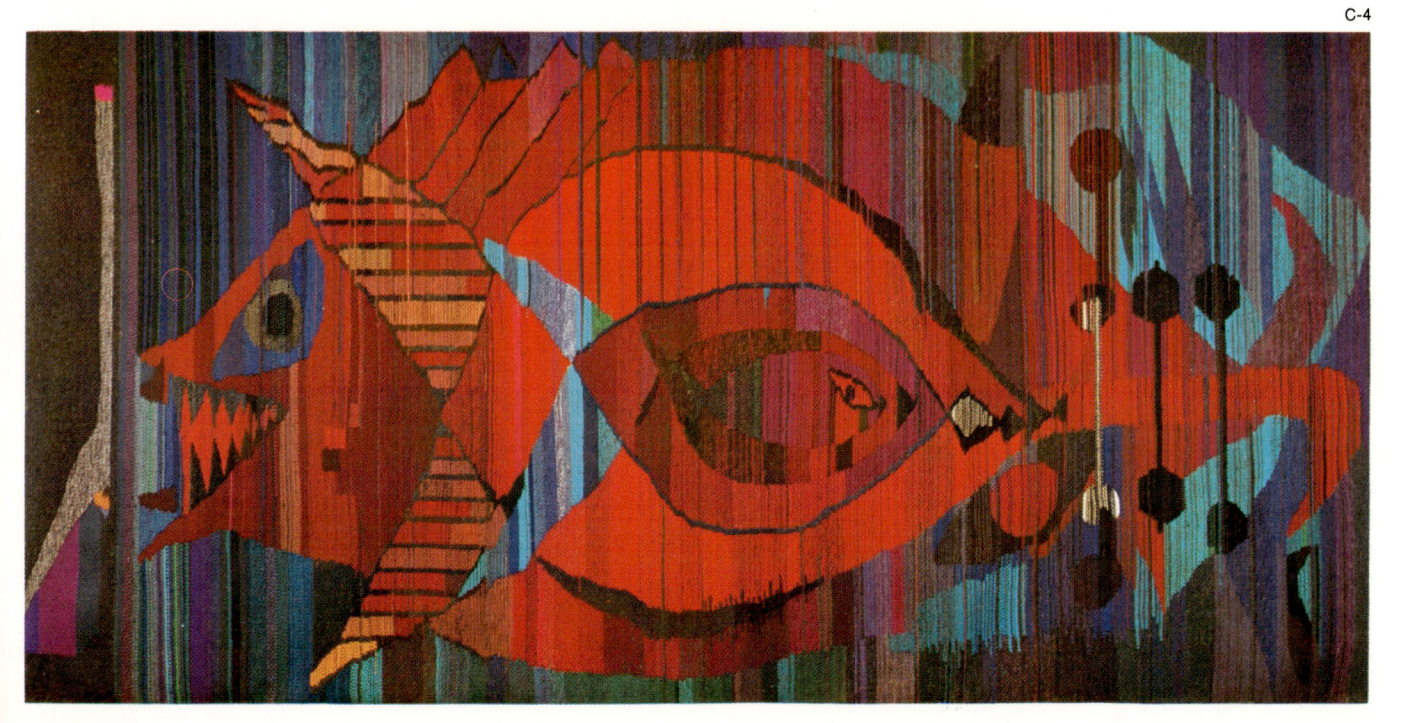

C-4

C-5

C-5. "Kirikko," rya in wool, 140 by 200 centimeters. By Terttu Tonero of Finland. (Courtesy of the Finnish Design Center and Osakeyhtio Neovius.)

C-6a and b. Ikat warp in wool. Weaving on the left (a) by Ulla Fornpeus of Sweden; one on the right (b) by Lotta Rudman of Sweden. (Courtesy of Marta Rinde-Ramsback, Sweden.)

C-7. "Yo Tunturissa," Lapp raanu by Elsa Montell-Saanio of Finland.

C-8. "Ruska," Lapp raanu by Elsa Montell-Saanio of Finland.

45

C-9

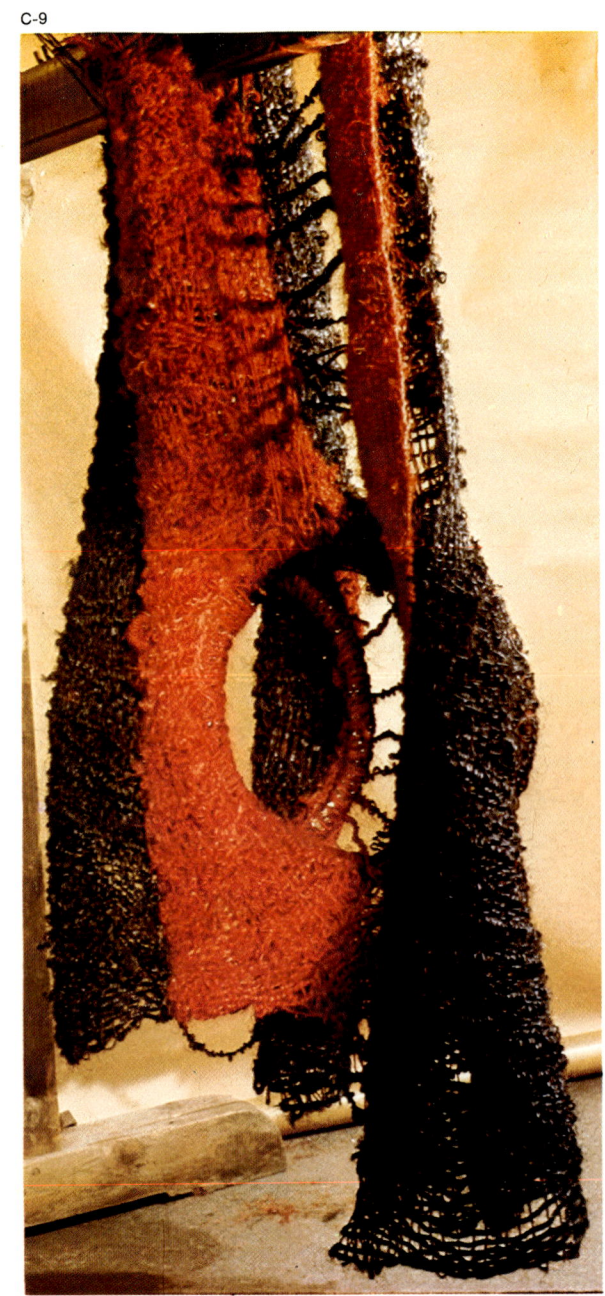

C-10

C-11

C-9. Sisal sculpture by Kari Jorgensen of Norway.

C-10. "Thread" by Mette Ussing of Denmark. Piece is done in double-weave with colored fish line.

C-11. Double-weave with pockets (detail) by Kirsten Dehlholm of Denmark.

C-12. "Fugleguden," a bird-god by Mette Ussing of Denmark. Pieces done in double-weave with linen, and then sewn into three-dimensional form.

C-13. "Running Through" by Elsebet Rahlff of Norway. Polyester warp with wool and plastic, using the rya technique.

C-14. Double-weave with pockets (detail) by Kirsten Dehlholm of Denmark.

C-15. "The Touch" (detail) by Elsebet Rahlff of Norway.

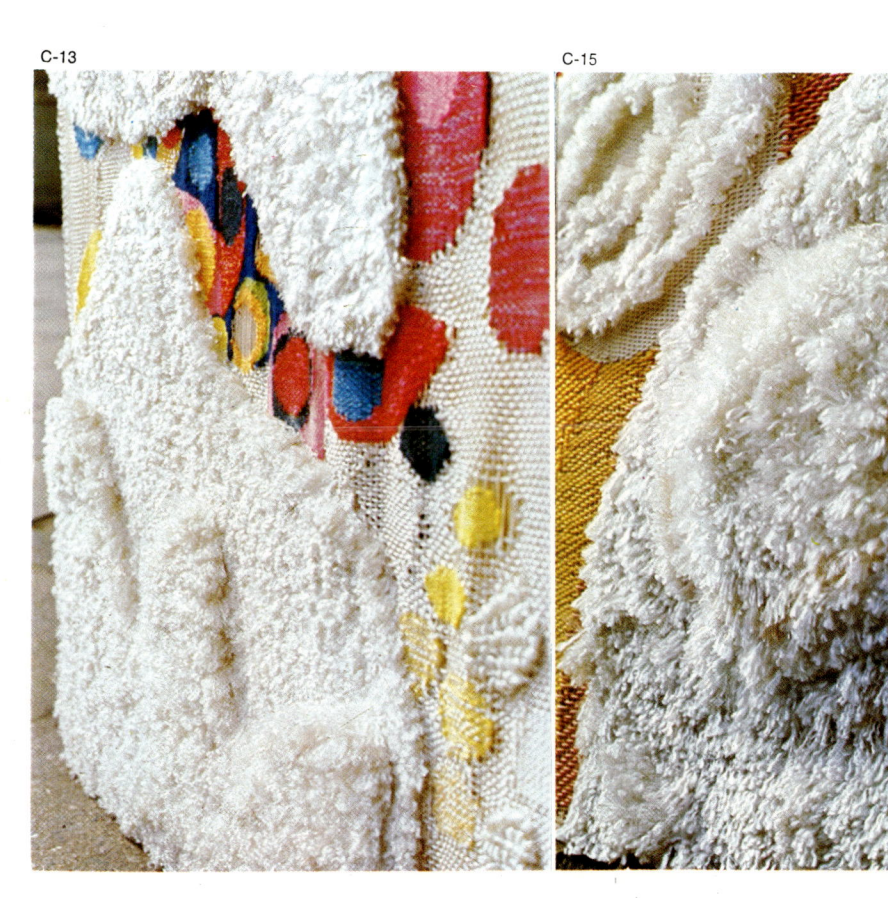

C-16. "Kryptos I" in damask and linen. By Dora Jung of Finland.

C-17. Woven dress by Ann-Mari Kornerup of Denmark. (Courtesy of Den Permanente.)

# RYA

1. Knotting the rya shag to the warp. (Courtesy of the National Museum of Finland.)

2. Here the rya tuffs are separated into bunches by color before being knotted. (Courtesy of Elsa Montell-Saanio of Finland.)

3. A row of rya knots are checked for color and tension before throws of the weft are made. (Courtesy of Elsa Montell-Saanio of Finland.)

4. "Tree of Life," wool rya dated 1794. (Courtesy of the National Museum of Finland.)

5. Rya tufts. (Courtesy of Metsovaara Oy of Finland.)

6. "Winter," rya of worsted wool, designed by Leena-Kaisa Halme. (Courtesy of Helsingin Villakehraamo of Finland.)

7. Early nineteenth-century wool rya. (Courtesy of the National Museum of Finland.)

8. "Sinetti," or "Seal," wool rya by Maija-Liisa Forss-Heinonen. (Courtesy of Helmi Vuorelma of Finland.)

9. Wool rya by Eva Brummer and Friends of Finnish Handicrafts. (Courtesy of the Finnish Society of Crafts and Design.)

10. "Dreams" by Sophie De Knoop of Sweden. The material is wool, and the frames around the design were done in the rya technique with black yarn. (Courtesy of Marta Rinde-Ramsback.)

11. "Universe," Dralon rya by Lea Thil-Junnila of Finland. Measures 120 by 180 centimeters. (Courtesy of the Bayer Chemical Company.)

12. "Indian Summer," Dralon rya by Oili Maki of Finland. Measures 150 by 210 centimeters. (Courtesy of the Bayer Chemical Company.)

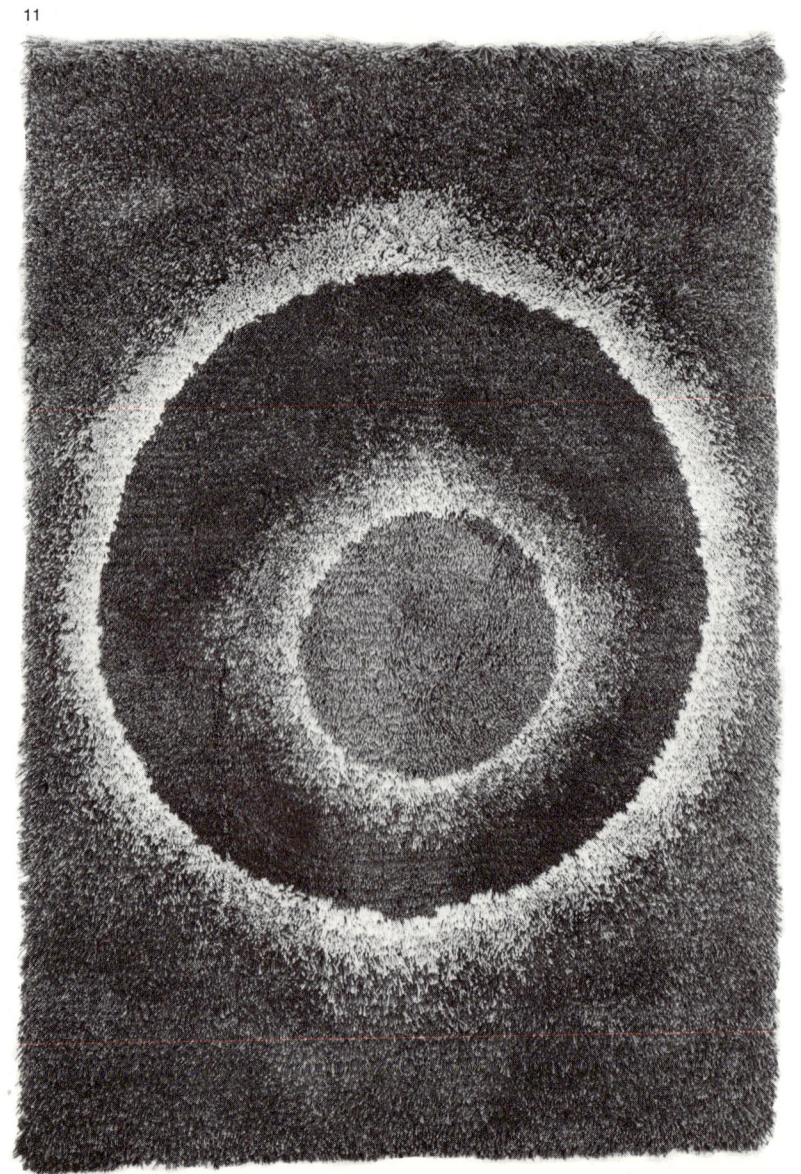

12

13a–q. Knots used in the rya technique. Figure g is the most commonly used. Other drawings illustrate varieties within the technique and group arrangements. (Illustrations by Sandy Willcox, courtesy of *The Ryijy Rugs of Finland* by U. T. Sirelius, published by Otava Publishing.)

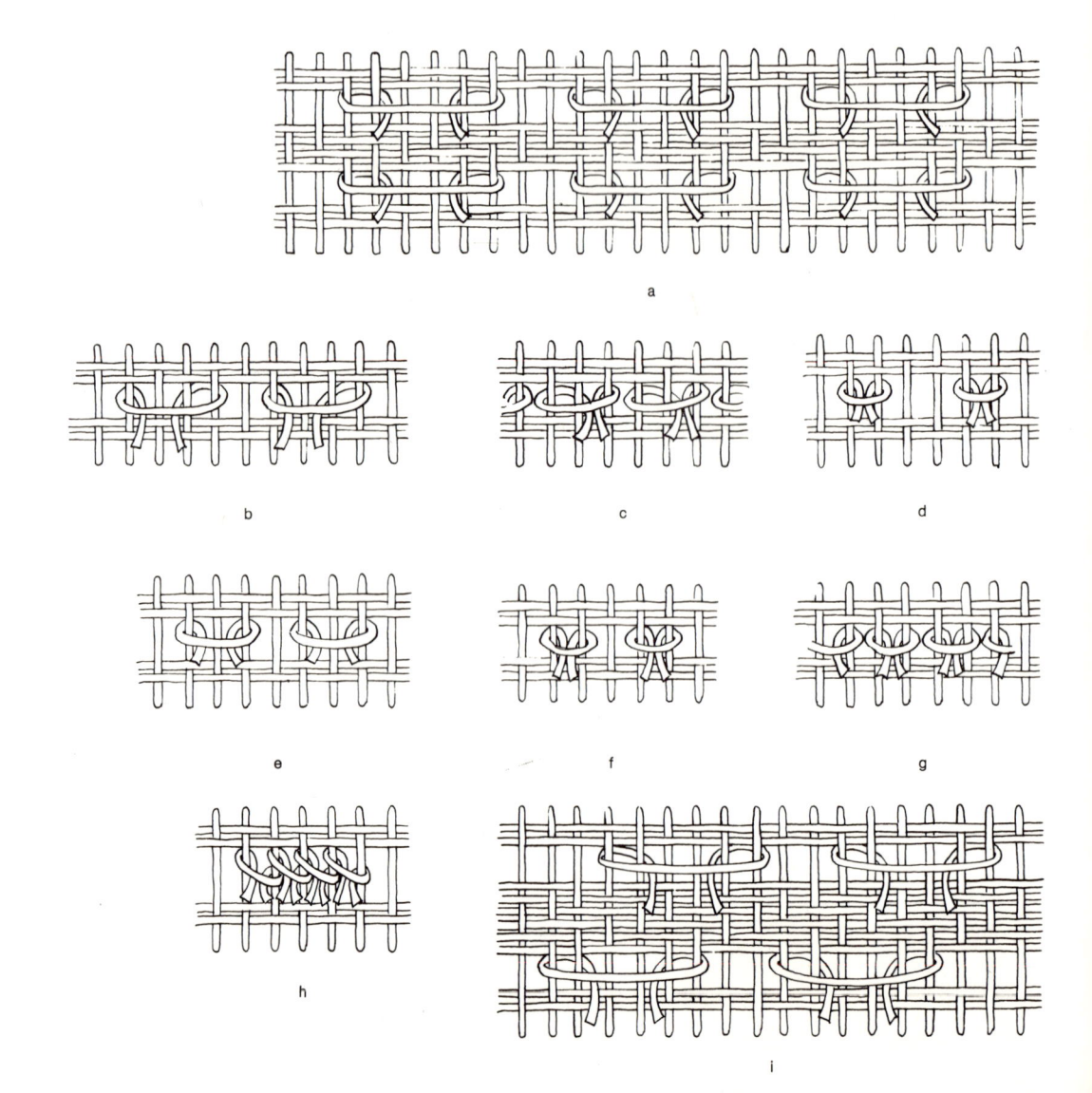

j

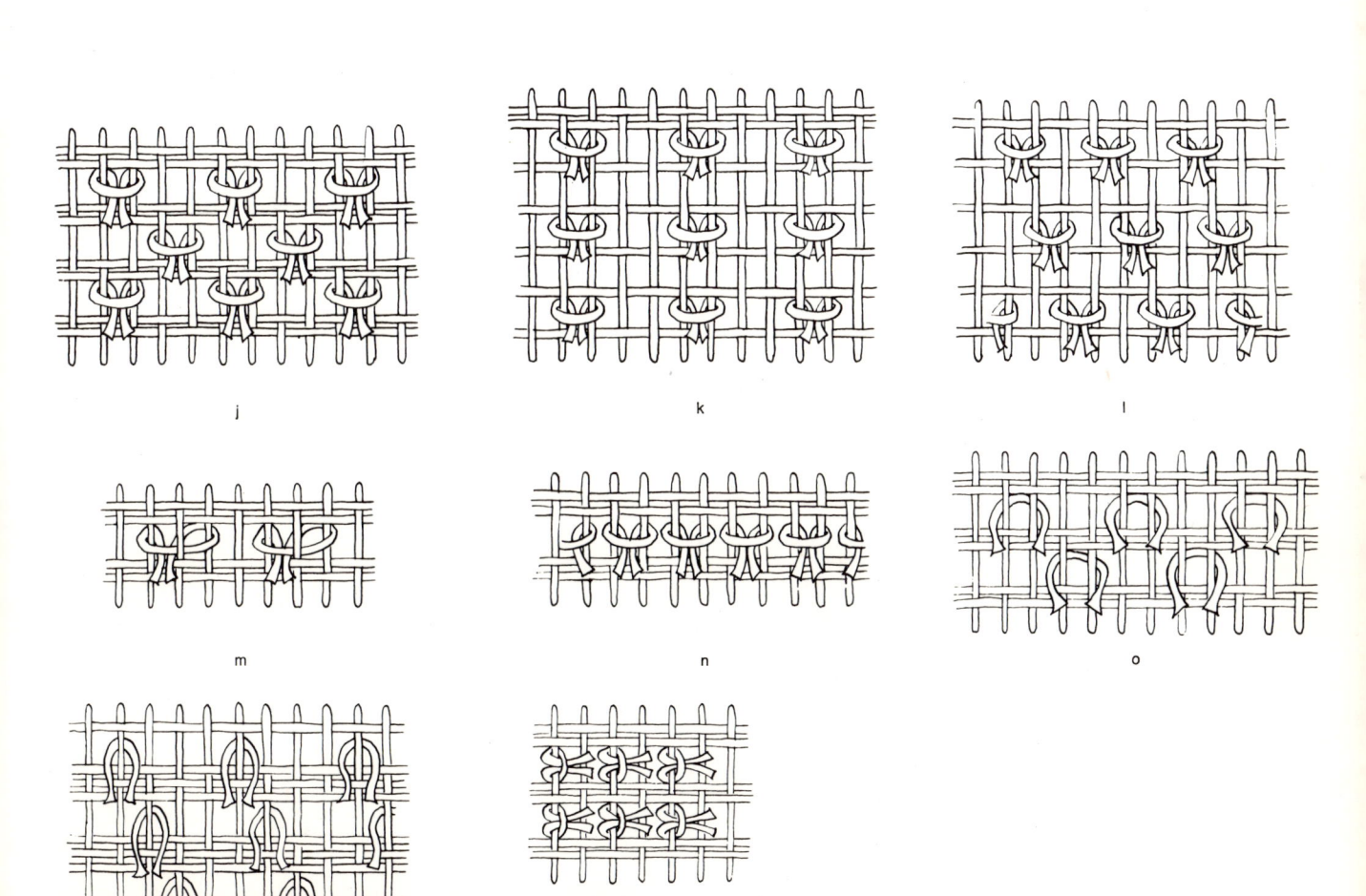

k

l

m

n

o

p

q

55

14. The rya will harmonize with objects in a natural setting. (Courtesy of Finnrya Oy and the Finnish Design Center.)

15. The "living" surface of the rya against the sea. (Courtesy of Finnrya Oy and the Finnish Design Center.)

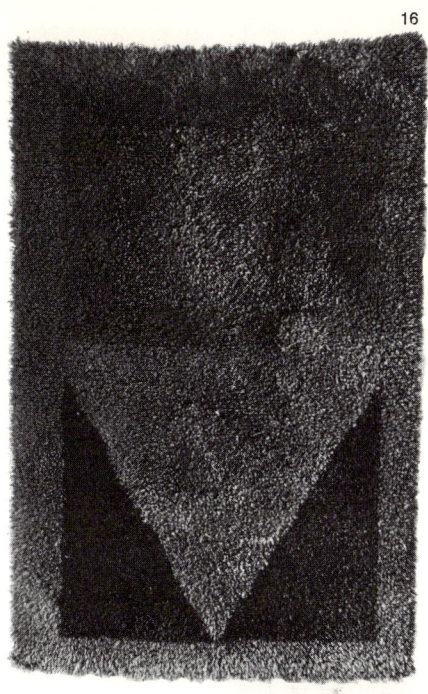

16. "Triangle," wool rya by Irja Mikkola. Piece measures 120 by 160 centimeters. (Courtesy of *Avotakka* magazine.)

17. Rya by Ulla Norvell of Sweden. (Courtesy of Marta Rinde-Ramsback.)

# DOUBLE-WEAVE

18. Linen double-weave by Maija Kolsi-Makela of Finland. This piece measures 100 by 170 centimeters and is woven in white, black, and red. (Courtesy of Helmi Vuorelma.)

19. "Smaragdsøen," double-weave wall hanging by Nana Nissen of Denmark. This piece in relief measures 5 by 52 by 138 centimeters and is woven wool yarn draped over a wooden dowel. Colored beads have been appliquéd to the back surface. (Courtesy of Den Permanente.)

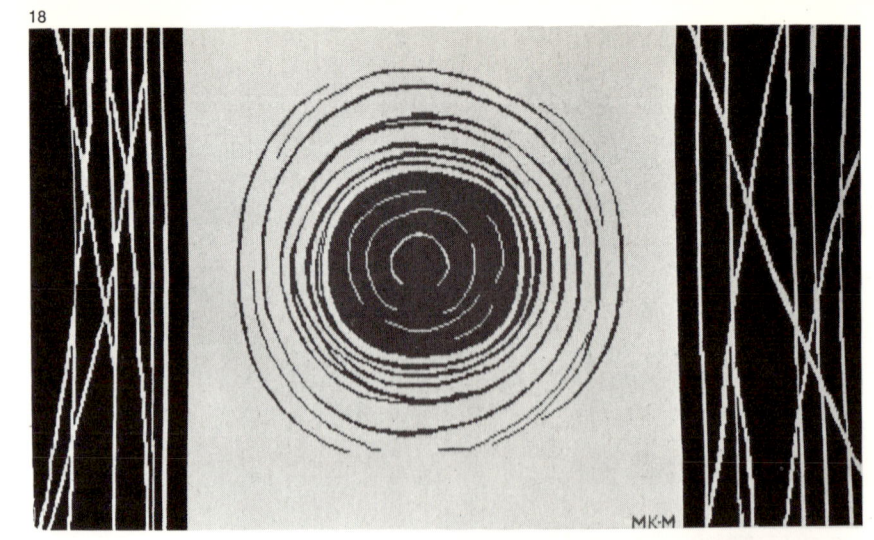

20. "Lonely Soul," linen double-weave by Anja Paloheimo of Finland, measures 70 by 240 centimeters. (Courtesy of Helmi Vuorelma.)

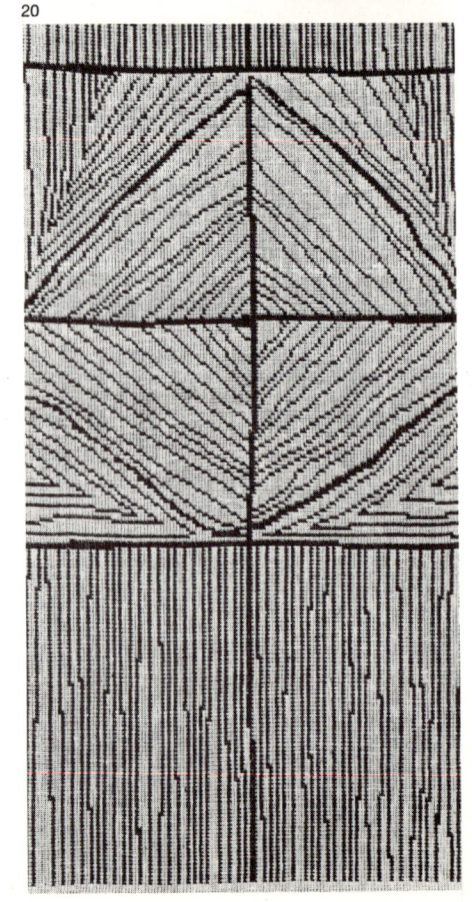

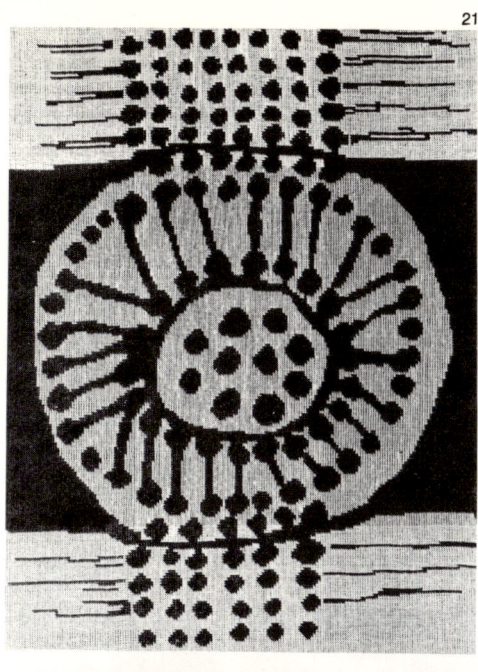

21. "Ring," linen double-weave by Raija Gripenberg of Finland, measures 95 by 125 centimeters. (Courtesy of Helmi Vuorelma.)

22. "Merimiehen Uni," linen double-weave by Maija-Liisa Forss-Heinonen of Finland. Design is in tones of gray and blue and measures 55 by 65 centimeters. (Courtesy of Helmi Vuorelma.)

23. Double-weave with pockets by Kirsten Delholm of Denmark. The warp and weft are both transparent plastic woven into pockets and filled with onion skin, feathers, plastic, yarn, raw wool, and ink stains on napkin.

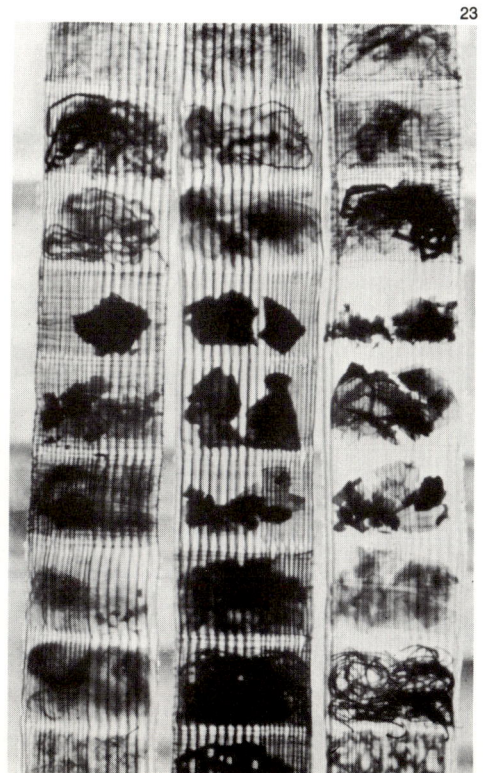

24. "Pesa," linen double-weave by Pirkko Hammarberg of Finland.

25. "Leva," linen double-weave by Pirkko Hammarberg of Finland.

26. Linen double-weave by Aini Suomi of Finland. This is an excellent example of how well the double-weave technique adapts itself to abstract, hard-edge imagery.

27. Double-weave wall hanging by Elsa Montell-Saanio of Finland. Piece measures 1 by 6 meters and hangs in the community center in Rovaniemi, Finland.

28. Detail of double-weave wall hanging by Elsa Montell-Saanio.

61

29. "The Reckoning," double-weave in black and white by Elsa Montell-Saanio of Finland. Piece measures 130 by 180 centimeters.

30. "Difficulty of Living," double-weave in black and white by Elsa Montell-Saanio of Finland. Measures 130 by 180 centimeters.

31. "Many Dwellings" by Annelie Machschefes of Sweden. Double-weave technique using wool warp and linen weft. Measures approximately 55 by 75 centimeters.

32. "Dandelion Girls" by Annelie Machschefes of Sweden. Double-weave technique in wool yarn.

33. "Dandelion Boys" by Annelie Machschefes of Sweden. Double-weave technique in vegetable-dyed wool yarn. Measures approximately 75 by 97 centimeters.

34. "Beach Alder" by Tellervo Strommer of Finland. Double-weave technique in yellow, green, and blue wool yarns. Measures 48 by 125 centimeters. (Courtesy of Wetterhoff.)

35. "Hiidenkirnu," double-weave by Maija-Liisa Forss-Heinonen. (Courtesy of Helmi Vuorelma of Finland.)

36. "Riikinkukko," double-weave by Maija-Liisa Forss-Heinonen of Finland. Linen measures 115 by 220 centimeters. (Courtesy of Helmi Vuorelma.)

# DAMASK

37. "Line Play," linen damask tablecloth by Dora Jung of Finland. (Courtesy of Tampella and the Finnish Design Center.)

38. Detail of damask technique in linen. (Courtesy of Dora Jung.)

39. "Shell" by Dora Jung of Finland. This piece is woven damask with linen warp and weft. (Courtesy of the Finnish Design Center.)

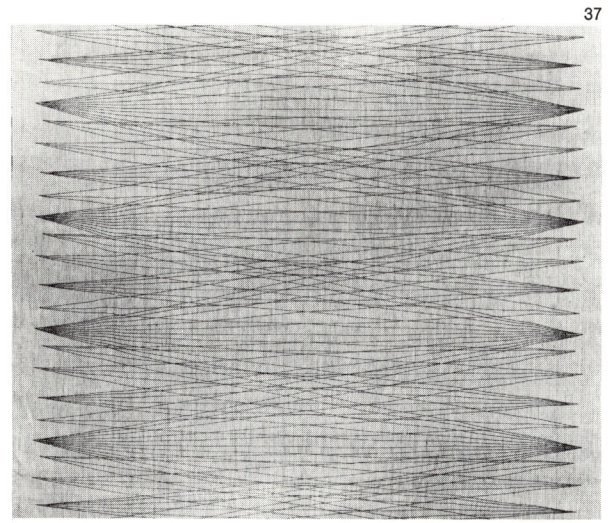

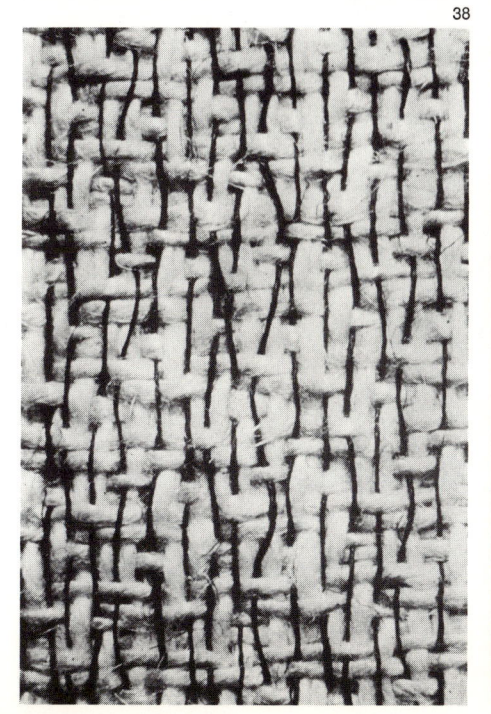

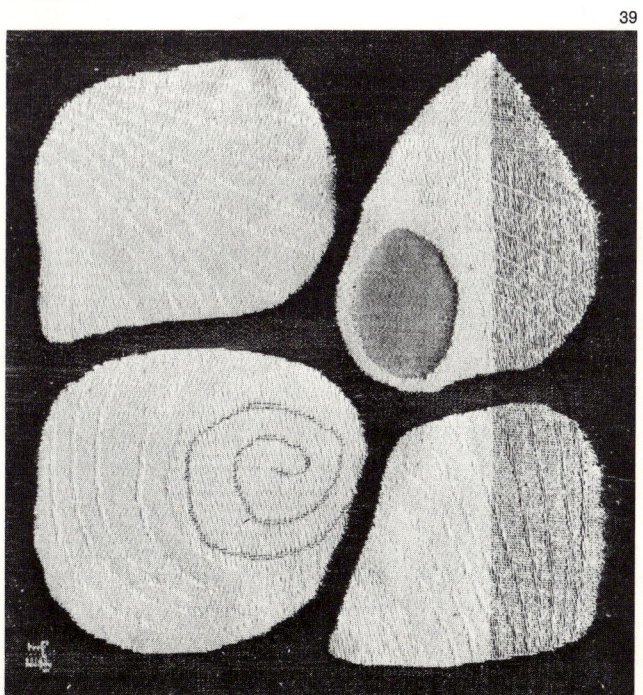

40. "Katarina Jagellonica," linen damask wall hanging by Dora Jung of Finland.

41. "Wild Ducks" in linen damask by Dora Jung of Finland. (Courtesy of the Finnish Ministry of Foreign Affairs.)

42. Detail of damask technique in linen. (Courtesy of Dora Jung.)

43. "Finnskog" by Dora Jung of Finland. Damask technique in linen.

# RAANU

44. "Rakotuli" by Elsa Montell-Saanio of Finland. Lapp raanu with characteristic horizontal stripes measures 120 by 180 centimeters. Material is wool.

45. Detail of raanu technique. (Courtesy of Elsa Montell-Saanio of Finland.)

46. The raanu was originally used for the Lapp *kota*, or teepee. The warp and weft braids were used to tie separate pieces together to form one large cone. (Courtesy of the National Museum of Finland.)

47. Inside kota. Note raanu stripes on the walls. (Courtesy of the National Museum of Finland.)

# ROSENGANG

48. "The American Eagle" by Helen Barynina of Sweden. Rosengang woven with wool, rayon, and plastic sequence. Measures 70 by 140 centimeters. (Courtesy of the National Museum, Stockholm.)

49. Bed cover in loose rosengang measuring 117 by 174 centimeters. Linen warp is twisted to the left, 37 threads to each 10 centimeters; weft threads contain cow hair, twisted to the right, and unbleached linen, two-ply, twisted to the left. (Courtesy of Nordiska Museet, Stockholm.)

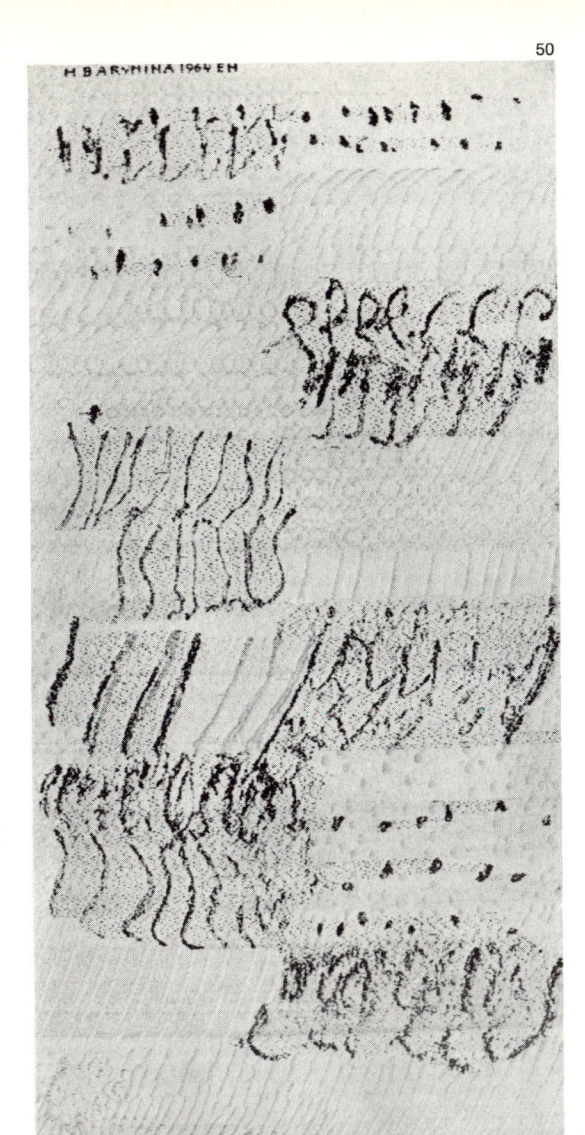

50. Detail of rosengang wall hanging entitled "Delta," by Helen Barynina of Sweden. Piece measures 2 by 4 meters. This is an example of how free calligraphy can be developed by hand-drawing picks loosely out across the warp. (Courtesy of the National Museum, Stockholm.)

51. Horse blanket in loose rosengang measures 134 by 195 centimeters. Cotton warp is twisted to the left, 70 threads to each 10 centimeters. Weft is wool yarn twisted to the left. (Courtesy of Nordiska Museet, Stockholm.)

52. Bed cover in loose rosengang measures 56 by 108 centimeters. Warp is fine linen, two-ply, twisted to the right, 36 threads to each 10 centimeters. Weft is two-ply wool and linen, twisted to the left. (Courtesy of Nordiska Museet, Stockholm.)

53. "Israel on the Gold Ground" by Annelie Machschefes of Sweden. On this piece, soumak, an ancient knotting technique, was combined with the rosengang. Piece measures approximately 125 by 150 centimeters.

54. "Israel on the Gold Ground" (detail) by Annelie Machschefes of Sweden.

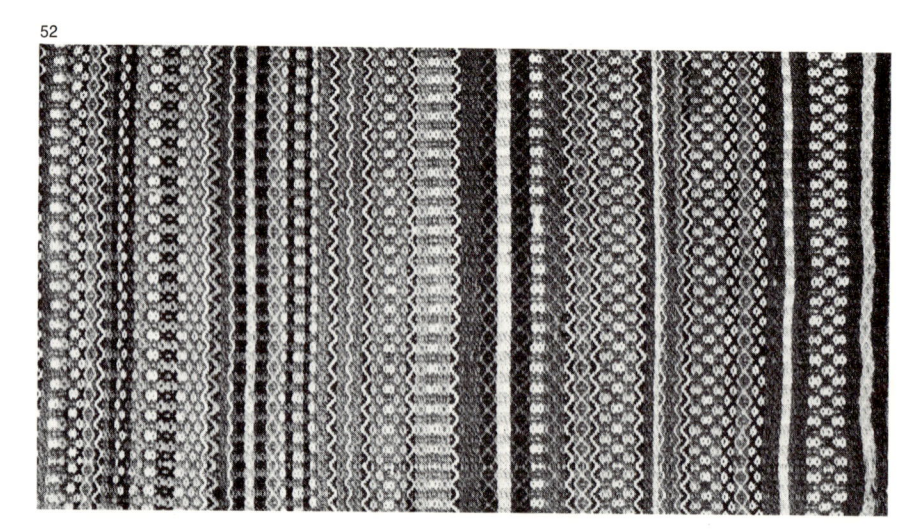

# WEAVING WITH A SELF-CONTAINED LOOM

69. "Globe" by Nana Nissen of Denmark is 80 centimeters in diameter. Wool yarn is woven over a frame of bamboo held together with wire. (Courtesy of Den Permanente.)

70. "Icosahedron" by Nana Nissen of Denmark. This mobile is woven over a frame of bamboo held together with wire. The yarn used is wool. (Courtesy of Den Permanente.)

71. Sculptured form looped and knotted around a core of wire. By Lone Brinch of Denmark. The material used is synthetic bast in light brown with glossy finish.

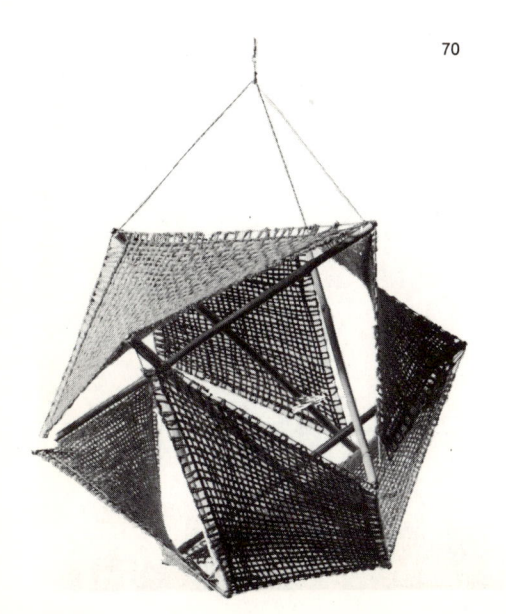

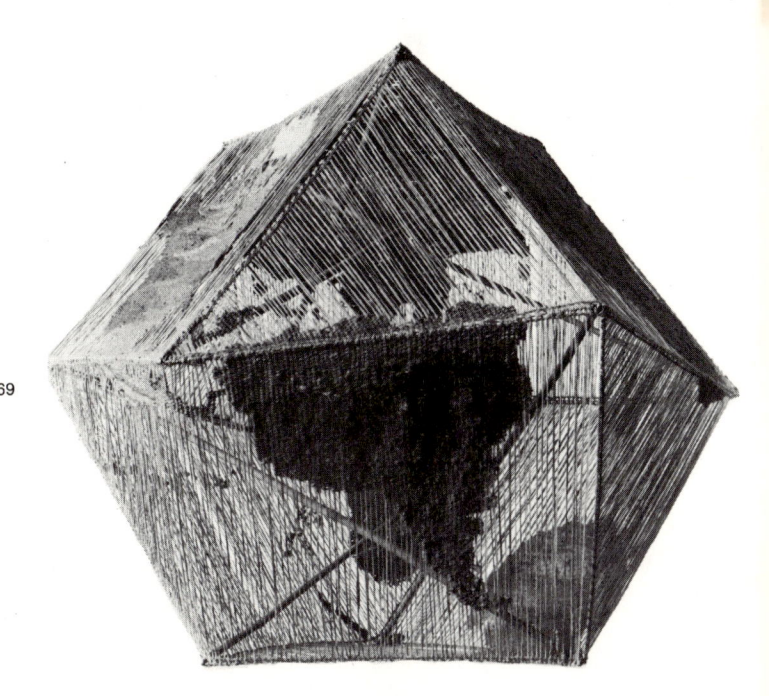

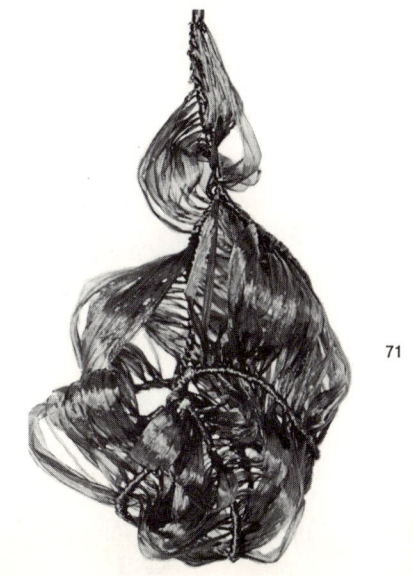

67. Skirt made from woven material, ikat-dyed. (Courtesy of the National Museum of Finland.)

68. Woven fabric after the warp was ikat-dyed. (Courtesy of the National Museum of Finland.)

# IKAT DYEING

64. Ikat stick with warp bound and ready for dyeing. (Courtesy of the National Museum of Finland.)

65. Detail of ikat stick showing warp wrapped around the dowel and tied at the pattern notch before dyeing. (Courtesy of the National Museum of Finland.)

66. Detail of ikat-dyed yarn after it has been used as a warp. The blocklike pattern developed in dyeing is clearly seen. (Courtesy of the National Museum of Finland.)

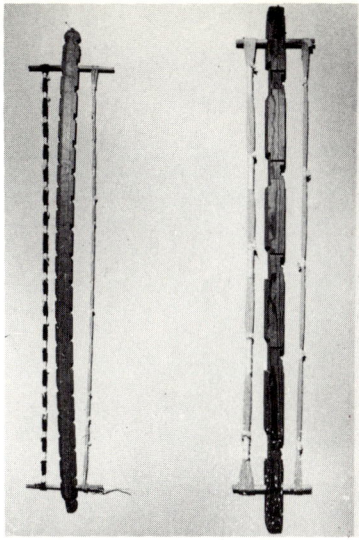

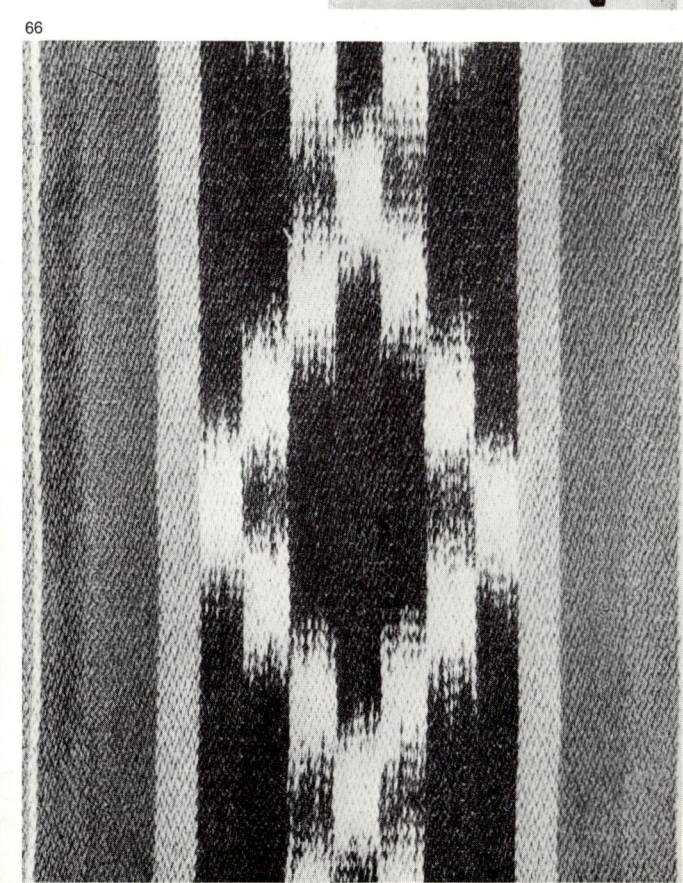

# FLAMSKVAVNAD

61. Chair cover in flamskvavnad technique, measures 45 by 47 centimeters. Linen warp twisted to the right, 50 threads to each 10 centimeters. Weft is wool, twisted to the right and left. (Courtesy of Nordiska Museet, Stockholm.)

62. Flamskvavnad carriage-seat cushion measuring 48 by 98 centimeters. Linen warp, 47 threads to each 10 centimeters. Weft is wool, and warp lines are toothed with 2 to 4 wefts. (Courtesy of Nordiska Museet, Stockholm.)

63. Seat cover in flamskvavnad measures 56 by 114 centimeters. Warp is linen, two-ply and twisted to the right, 25 threads to each 10 centimeters. Weft is wool, two-ply and twisted to the right. (Courtesy of Nordiska Museet, Stockholm.)

# ROLLAKAN

57. Rollakan technique in geometric pattern blocks. Detail is from a rug woven by Ann-Mari Forsberg of Marta Maas-Fjetterstrom Ab, Sweden. (Courtesy of the National Museum, (Stockholm.)

58. Carriage cushion in rollakan. The warp is linen, two-ply and twisted to the right, 42 threads to each 10 centimeters. The weft contains 2 to 3 threads of wool yarn, twisted to the right. Piece measures 48 by 89 centimeters. (Courtesy of Nordiska Museet, Stockholm.)

59. Bed cover in rollakan. Piece has a linen warp, 45 threads to each 10 centimeters, and measures 124 by 173 centimeters. (Courtesy of Nordiska Museet, Stockholm.)

60. Rollakan design by Barbro Nilsson of Sweden. (Courtesy of Svenska Slojdforeningen and Marta Maas-Fjetterstrom.)

55. "Saturday Evening" in rosengang with linen and wool. By Annelie Machschefes of Sweden. Piece measures approximately 75 by 105 centimeters.

56. Rosengang technique with wool and linen warp, and linen weft. By Annelie Machschefes of Sweden. Piece measures approximately 70 by 117 centimeters.

72. Close-up view of sculptured form by Lone Brinch of Denmark.

73. "With Open Eyes," high relief by Grete Balle of Denmark. This piece is woven in three layers, within a wooden, shadow-box frame. The piece is 55 by 67 centimeters. Front layer is woven with wire and coarse rope; the center layer is woven from interlaced strips of leather; and the back layer is a fine mesh chicken wire.

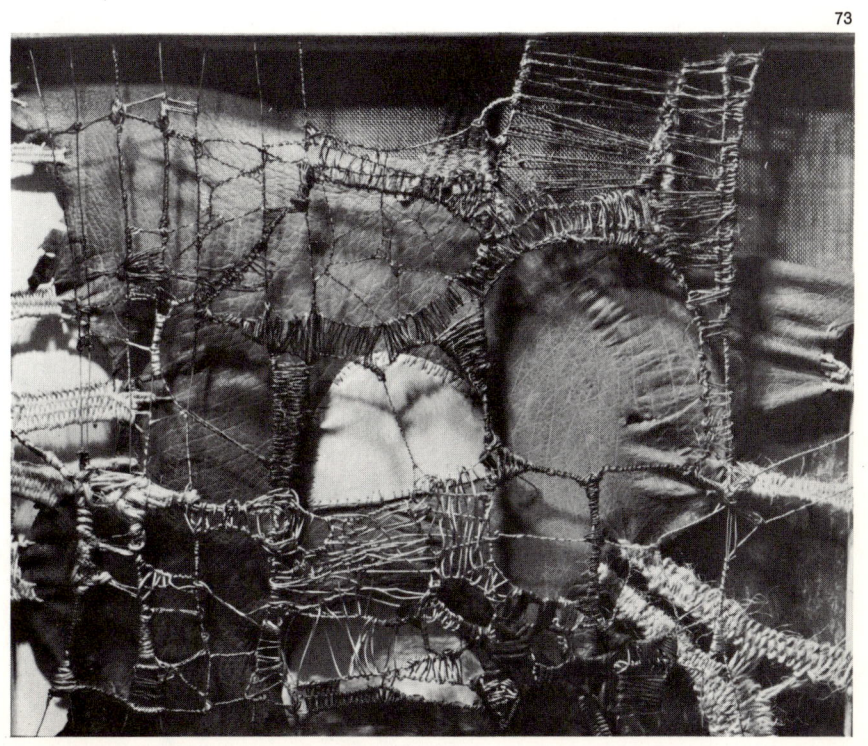

74. Wall hanging (front) by Helle Kaastrup-Olsen of Denmark. The piece was woven with sisal and tar yarn and then looped over a rectangular wooden frame. (Courtesy of the Danish Handicraft Guild.)

75. Wall hanging (side) by Helle Kaastrup-Olsen of Denmark. (Courtesy of Viggo Kragmann.)

76. "Curtain" by Bjorg Heggstad Jakhelln of Norway. This piece was woven on a frame to give it more freedom. The materials used are cotton and wool; the piece is 85 by 110 centimeters.

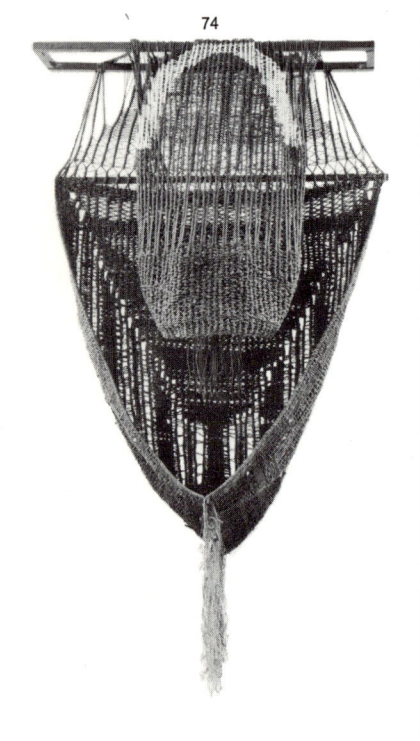

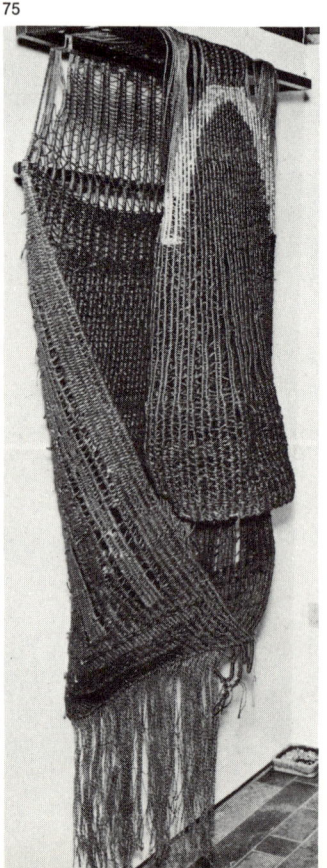

77. Close-up view of high relief by Grete Balle of Denmark.

78. Another view of "Curtain" by Bjorg Heggstad Jakhelln of Norway.

79. "Transparent Life" by Grete Balle of Denmark. A tree branch was used here as a self-contained loom. Into the frame were woven threads of wire, sisal, and leather. The piece is 25 by 25 centimeters.

80. "Living Stillness" by Grete Balle of Denmark. This piece is woven around a concealed frame made from iron rods. It includes sisal, leather, horsehair, rope and tar yarn.

81. "Living Stillness" (detail) by Grete Balle of Denmark.

82. "Happy Meeting" by Grete Balle of Denmark. Again, a tree branch was used as a self-contained loom, with woven threads of sisal, hemp, and leather.

83. "Happy Meeting" (detail) by Grete Balle of Denmark.

# SCULPTURE AND RELIEF

84. "Dark Foggy Figure" by Grete Balle of Denmark. Piece measures 65 by 165 centimeters and was formed by draping woven fabric over a lampshade, coating it with glue, and then leaving it to harden. After the lampshade was removed, the form supported itself. It was then painted.

85. "Brothers Strikker" by Kirsten Dehlholm of Denmark. The piece is intended either to be hung on a wall or from a ceiling, or draped over a chair. The major portion of the form was knitted from linen sailcloth. Mohair was also used.

86. "Brothers Strikker" (detail) by Kirsten Dehlholm of Denmark. The edges of this curled linen sailcloth were frayed by removing threads.

87. Mushroom relief by Kirsten Dehlholm of Denmark. The mushroom forms are built of loops left in the tow weft. Some of these loops were cut; others left uncut. The loops were bound and spliced the way rope is.

88. A second view of mushroom relief by Kirsten Dehlholm of Denmark. The material used in binding the weft loops included both bast and celluloid.

89. "Birds' Nests" by Kirsten Dehlholm of Denmark. Each nest form was first knitted and then sewn together into full forms. The piece is suspended from a tree branch. Material includes mohair, synthetic bast, and plastic bags cut in strips.

90. "Birds' Nests" (detail) by Kirsten Dehlholm of Denmark.

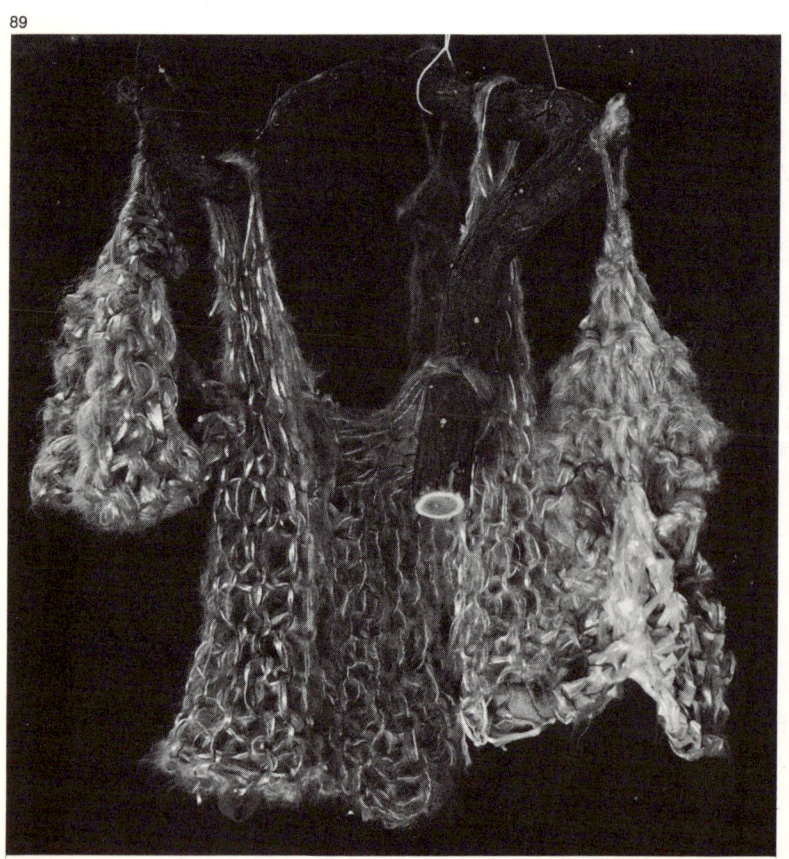

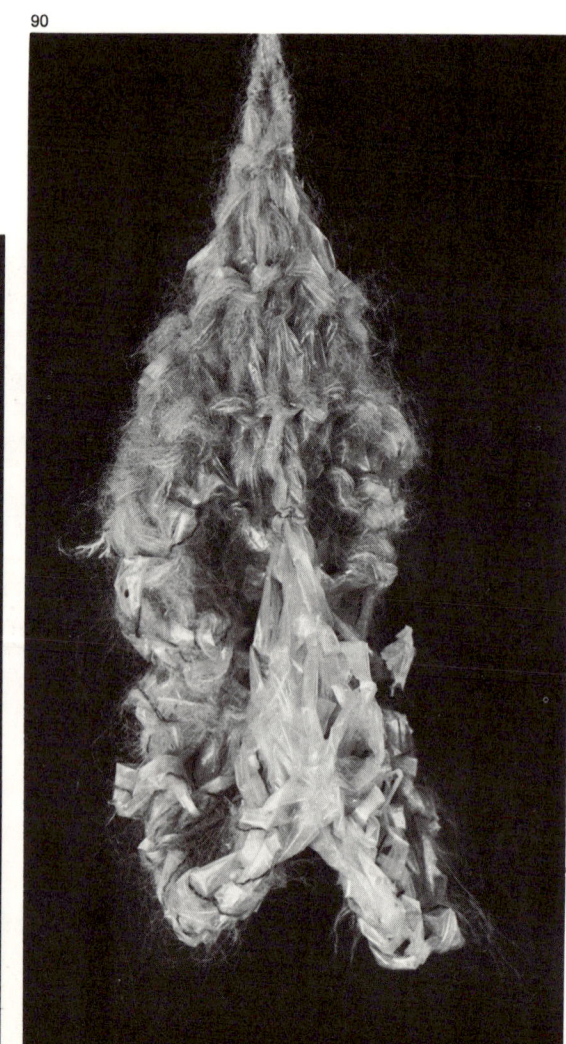

91. "Tradkuppel" by Jette Gemzoe of Denmark. This piece combines macramé knotting, glass balls, and plastic. It is suspended from a ceiling.

92. "Tradkuppel" (detail) by Jette Gemzoe of Denmark.

93. "Octopus" by Kristina Bang of Denmark. This piece was made to be used as a prop in a children's theater. The core is made from a discarded umbrella. Nylon stockings were filled with small bits of colored foam rubber and then sewn onto the umbrella spokes. The eye of the octopus was made from papier-mâché. Between the suspended octopus arms, a netlike form was woven.

94. "A Portrait," white on white, by Elisabet Hasselberg-Olsson of Sweden. It measures 65 by 70 centimeters. The material is white linen, and the relief is made with thread ties.

95. "Ausigt" by Helle Kaastrup-Olsen of Denmark. It measures 90 by 140 centimeters and is made from sisal, tar yarn, and hair from a St. Bernard dog.

96. "Nympho" by Helle Kaastrup-Olsen of Denmark. Piece is made from sisal and measures 110 by 130 centimeters.

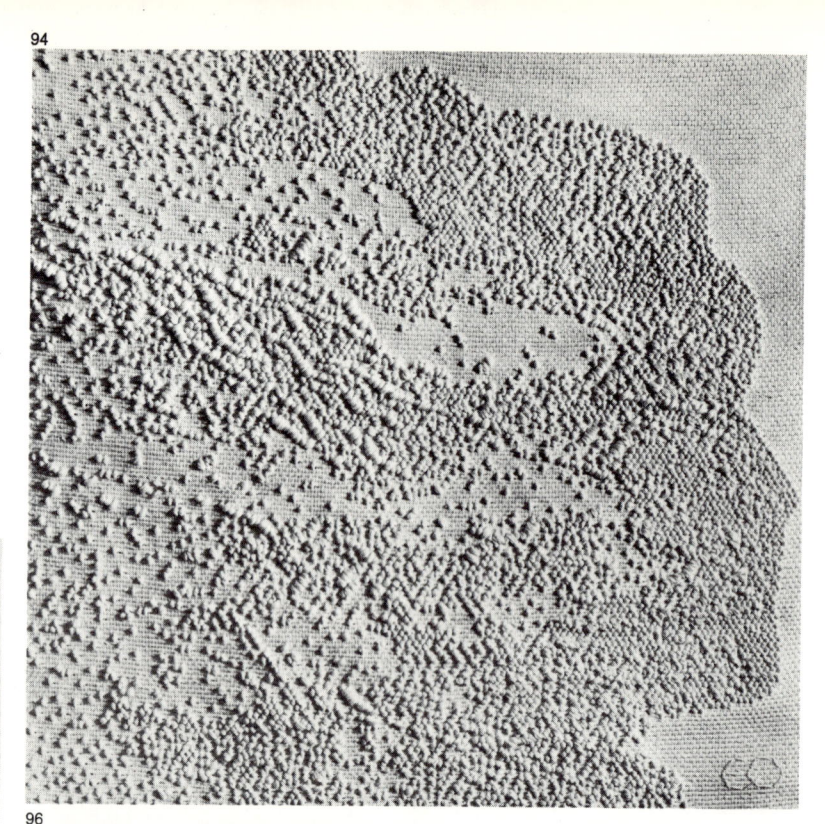

97. Wall hanging by Jette Gemzoe of Denmark. (Courtesy of the Danish Society of Arts, Crafts, and Industrial Design.)

98. "Nympho" (detail) by Helle Kaastrup-Olsen of Denmark.

99. "Growing Plants" by Naja Salto of Denmark. (Courtesy of the Danish Society of Arts, Crafts, and Industrial Design.)

100. "Bird Cage for a Cardinal" by Oili Maki of Finland. Made of wool.

101. Detail of wall hanging by Naja Salto of Denmark. The piece uses hand-spun wool, rya yarn, bast, and sisal.

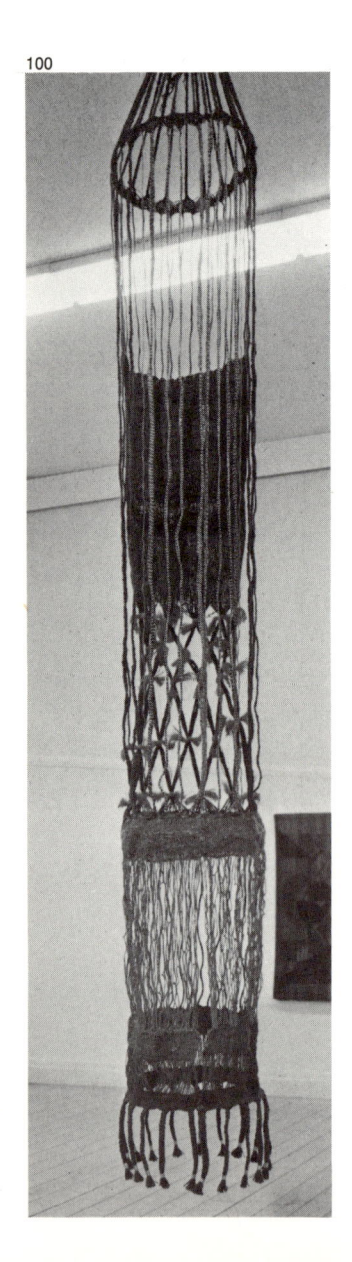

102. "Knot" by Mette Ussing of Denmark. Materials are linen, cotton, and wool, all in white. The knot is a continuous, unbroken form without a seam. After the length of the knot was woven, the warp threads within the knot were removed from the loom, knotted, and then replaced on the loom. (Courtesy of the Danish Society of Arts, Crafts, and Industrial Design.)

103. Nontraditional rya knotting by Bodil Bodtker-Naess of Denmark. Sheep hair, naturally spun, was knotted in the rya technique against a woven background of wool and linen.

104. Rya knots used to build relief by Franka Rasmussen of Denmark. (Courtesy of the Danish Society of Arts, Crafts, and Industrial Design.)

105. "Space Roses" (detail) by U-B Emitslof-Dejmo of Sweden. (Courtesy of Svenska Slojdforeningen.)

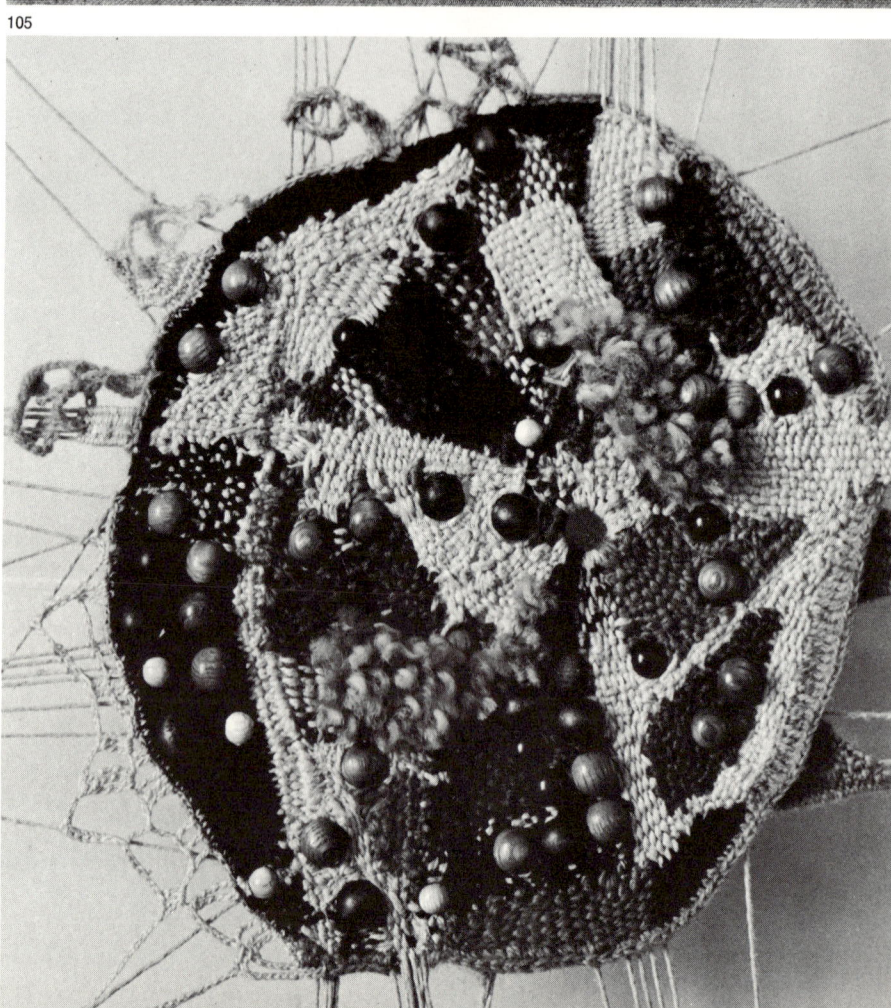

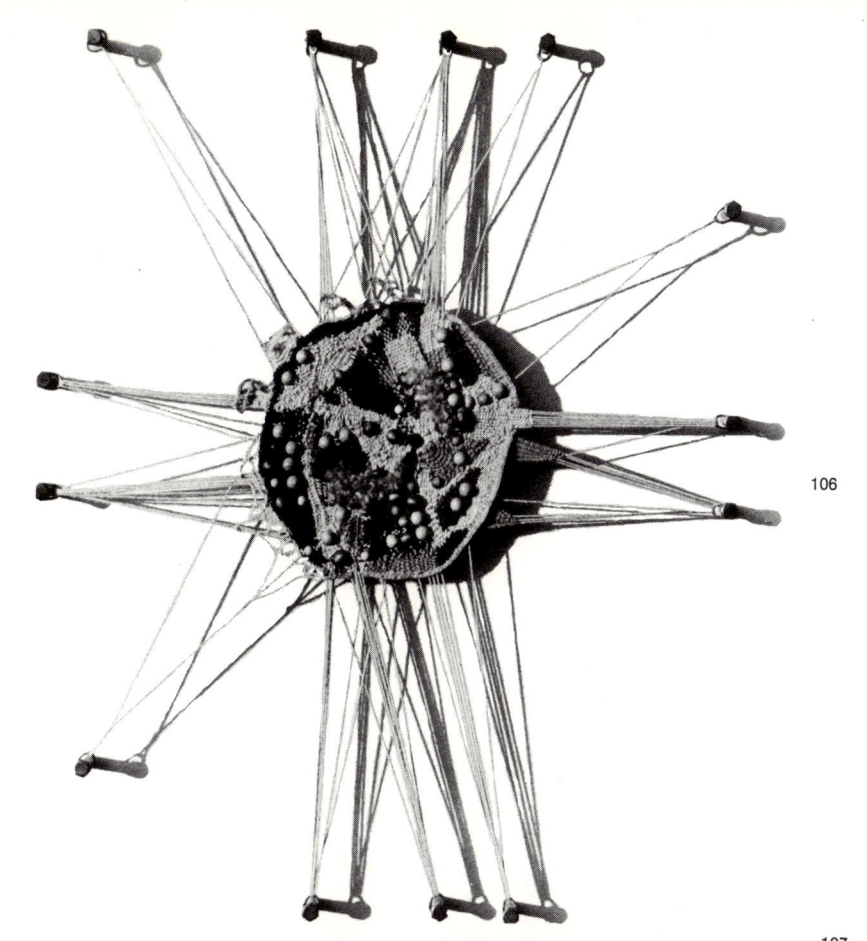

106. "Space Roses" by U-B Emitslof-Dejmo of Sweden. This is one of several similar relief forms attached over a larger background of plain weaving. The overall piece measures 600 by 1300 centimeters.

107. Rya knots used loosely against wool to build relief by Franka Rasmussen of Denmark. (Courtesy of the Danish Society of Arts, Crafts, and Industrial Design.)

108. "Pampula" by Marjatta Metsovaara of Finland. Woven in soft wool.

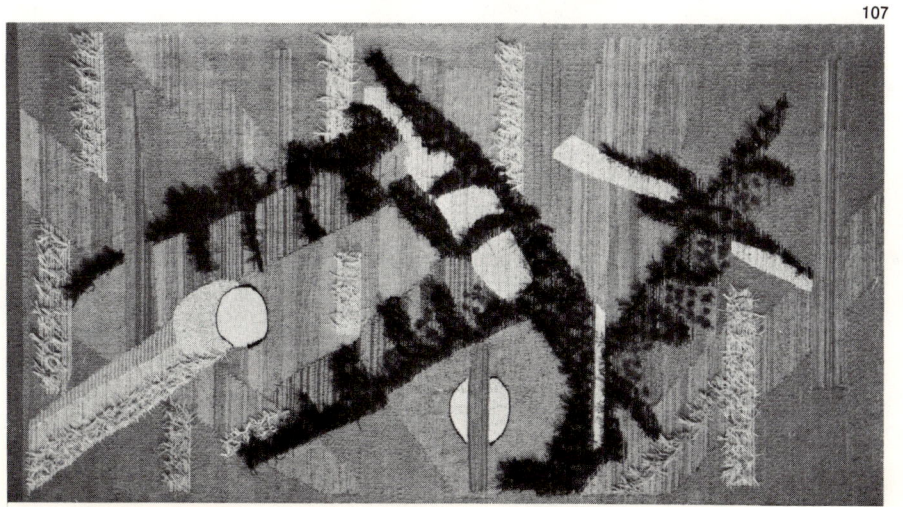

109. Detail of surface texture by Naja Salto of Denmark. (Courtesy of the Danish Society of Arts, Crafts, and Industrial Design.)

110. "Experiment" by Age Faith-Ell of Sweden. Background is linen, foreground is cotton.

# WALL HANGINGS

111. "Red Crocus" by Ann-Mari Lindbom of Sweden. (Courtesy of Svenska Slojdforeningen and Marta Maas-Fjetterstrom.)

112. "Cock and Hen" by Maud Hugo of Sweden. (Courtesy of Svenska Slojdforeningen.)

113. "Nightly Cult Center" by Hans Krondahl of Sweden. Piece is comprised of woven applications. (Courtesy of Svenska Slojdforeningen.)

114. Hair-yarn rug by Monalill Larsson of Sweden. (Courtesy of Svenska Slojdforeningen.)

115. Wall hanging by Annelie Machschefes of Sweden. Linen warp with wool and linen weft.

116. "In the Underground," wool and linen, by Annelie Machschefes of Sweden.

117. "Inscription Vietnam" by Elisabet Hasselberg-Olsson of Sweden. This piece is white on white, a study in light and contrast. The material is hand-twisted, bleached linen, which develops free cracks on the surface. Everything but the tiny embroidered flowers was done right on the loom. It measures 90 by 180 centimeters.

118. Wall hanging by Franka Rasmussen of Denmark. (Courtesy of the Danish Society of Arts, Crafts, and Industrial Design.)

119. Wall hanging by Lea Tennberg of Finland. Materials are bleached and unbleached, hand-spun linen. (Courtesy of the Finnish Society of Crafts and Design.)

120. Wall hanging by Lea Tennberg of Finland. Bleached and unbleached hand-spun linen woven in joined strips. (Courtesy of the Finnish Society of Crafts and Design.)

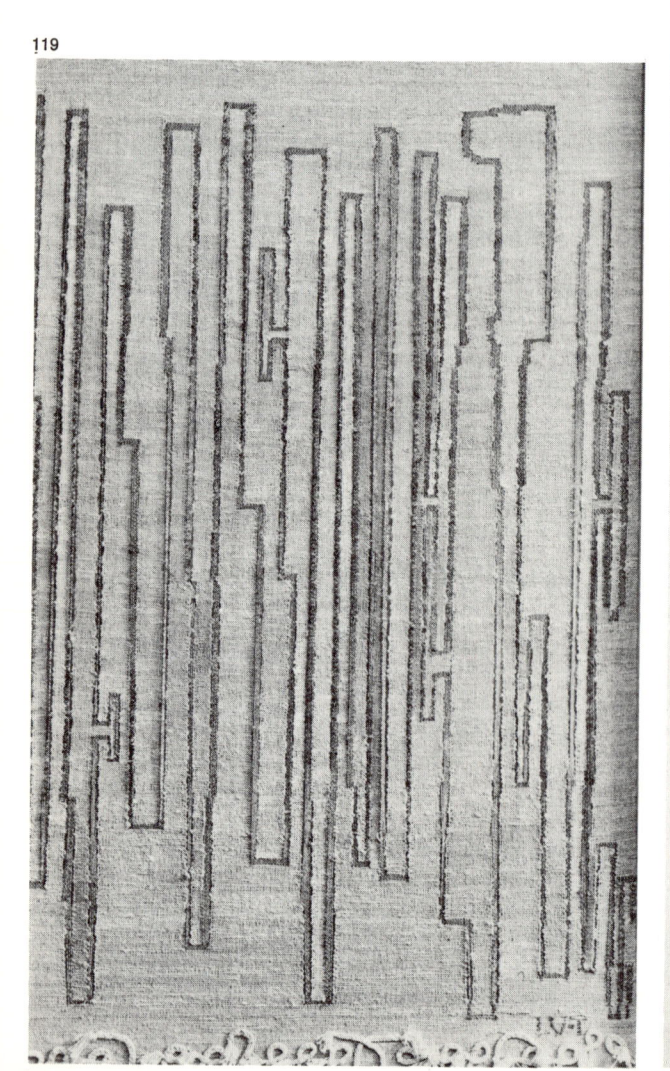

121. "Spring Blossoms" by Lea Tennberg of Finland. It measures 24 by 100 centimeters and is bleached and unbleached, hand-spun linen with commercial linen.

122. "Industrial Suburb," triptych by Lea Tennberg of Finland. It measures 2 by 3 meters and is made from commercial linen in 20 different colors, as well as from bleached and unbleached hand-spun linen.

123. "Zeus II" by Irja Mikkola of Finland. It is all wool and measures 130 by 155 centimeters. (Courtesy of Avotakka.)

124. Wall hanging by Asger Jorn of Denmark. (Courtesy of the Danish Society of Arts, Crafts, and Industrial Design.)

125. Wall hanging by Margareta Ahlstedt-Willandt of Finland. (Courtesy of the Finnish Society of Crafts and Design.)

126. "Zeus" by Irja Mikkola of Finland. It is wool and measures 125 by 175 centimeters. (Courtesy of Avotakka.)

127. "Yellow Melon" by Ann-Mari Forsberg of Sweden. (Courtesy of Svenska Slojdforeningen and Marta Maas-Fjetterstrom.)

128. Wall hanging, 1½ by 3½ meters, by Helle Kaastrup-Olsen of Denmark. Materials include sisal, wool, nylon, and linen.

129. Wall hanging by Ingegerd and Carl Bjerring of Denmark. (Courtesy of the Danish Society of Arts, Crafts, and Industrial Design.)

130. Wall hanging by Risse Berntsen of Denmark. (Courtesy of the Danish Society of Arts, Crafts, and Industrial Design.)

131. "Rosa og Oker" by Brit Fuglevaag Warsinski of Norway. Materials are linen, wool, and cotton.

132. Wall hanging by Kaisa Melanton of Sweden. (Courtesy of Svenska Slojdforeningen.)

133. "Gaudy Birds" by Marianne Richter of Sweden. (Courtesy of Svenska Slojdforeningen.)

134. "Chestnut" by Asa Bengtsson of Sweden. (Courtesy of Svenska Slojdforeningen.)

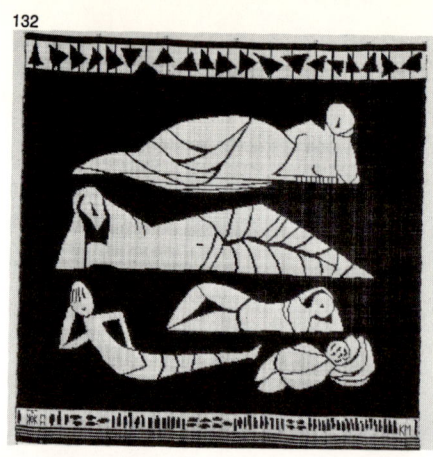

135. Wall hanging, 90 by 116 centimeters, by Jette Gemzoe of Denmark. Made of hand-spun wool and tar yarn. (Courtesy of the Danish Handicraft Guild.)

136. "Scroll" by Jette Gemzoe of Denmark. This piece is 1.60 by 2.40 meters and is made from hand-spun wool and tar yarn. It is looped over a dowel at each end so that the viewer can turn it to select his own picture. Two thicknesses are looped over the dowel, one inside the other. The outer piece contains three windows so the viewer can not only change the outside image, but can select the color within the window. The pattern was designed with no beginning and no end so that no matter how it is turned, there is always a composition in view.

137. Rya wall hanging, part of series entitled "Dreams." By Sophie De Knoop of Sweden. (Courtesy of Marta Rinde-Ramsback.)

138. Weaving by Danish children.

# UNUSUAL MATERIALS

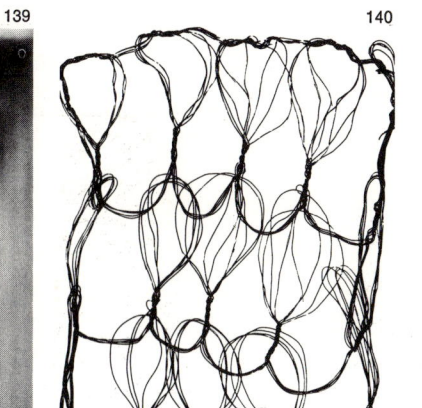

139. "Window Jewel" by Clara Salander of Sweden. The material is brass plate, with nylon and glass beads woven into the negative space. (Courtesy of Marta Rinde-Ramsback.)

140. An exercise in wire weaving without a loom. (Courtesy of Taideteollinen Oppilaitos, Finland.)

141. Wall hanging or room divider by Birgitta Mellentin of Denmark. This piece was made by knotting string, sisal, and tar yarn and then knotting lengths of brass tubing into place. Piece was begun vertically and knotted from the top down.

142. Detail of brass-tube wall hanging by Birgitta Mellentin of Denmark.

143. "Space Screen" by Puk Lippmann of Denmark. This is an example of weaving within a self-contained frame. The frame and some of the interior structure are made from soldered copper tubing. The form is shaped like an S and is intended as a room divider. A number of techniques are used in the piece, and the materials include copper, tow, unbleached wool, raffia, tar yarn, hemp, and nylon. It measures approximately 147 by 295 centimeters. (Courtesy of the Danish Handicraft Guild.)

144. "Space Screen" (detail) by Puk Lippmann of Denmark.

145. Wall hanging by Birgit Ullhammar of Sweden. This piece employs cable, rope, electric-light cord, and nylon warp. (Courtesy of the Form Design Center in Malmo.)

146. Detail of wall hanging by Birgit Ullhammar of Sweden.

147. Exercise in materials. Piece is woven with bud sprigs and hemp. (Courtesy of Taideteollinen Oppilaitos, Finland.)

148. Hanging by Siri Blackstad of Norway. The warp is a silver-like metal thread; the weft is almost clear plastic. Bleached, unspun linen hangs in relief down the front, and at the top there is a partially concealed mirror.

149. "Growth" by Kari Jorgensen of Norway. Piece is made from woven sisal and wire.

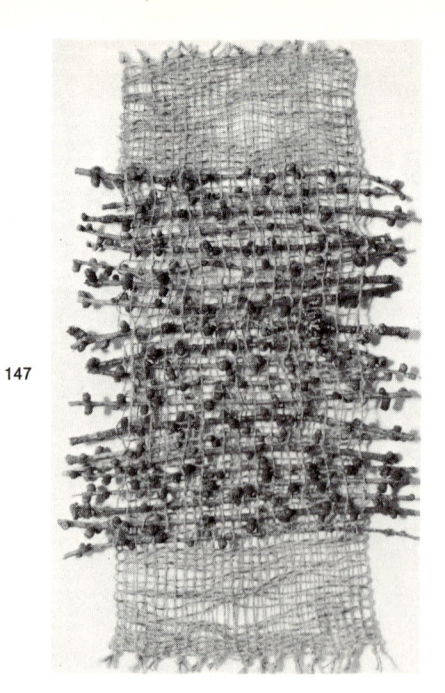

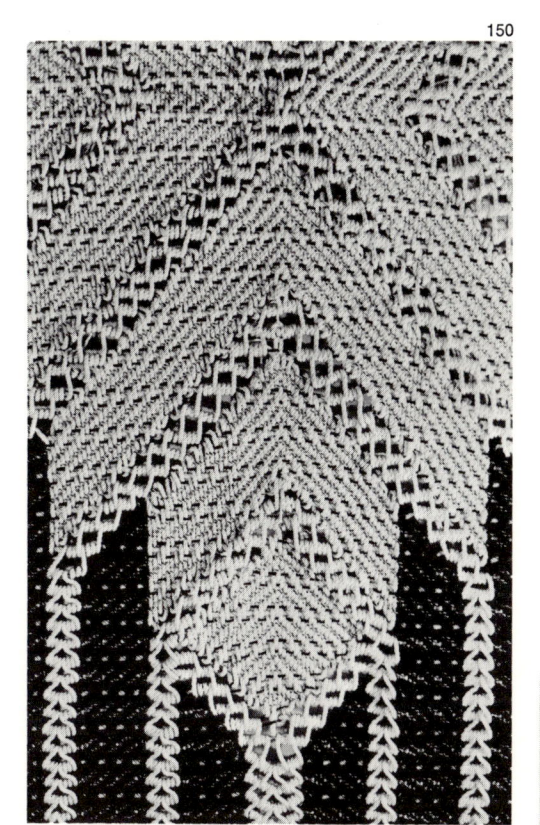

150. Detail of nylon wall hanging by Bodil Bodtker-Naess of Denmark.

151. Nylon wall hanging by Bodil Bodtker-Naess of Denmark. The piece combines nylon and jute and is stretched to hold tension between aluminum stretchers. The technique used is soumak, and the size of the piece is 2 by 3 meters.

152. "Stripe in Stripe" by Age Faith-Ell of Sweden. This is a thin but stiff textile woven with cotton and linen in contrasting white and black. (Courtesy of Eriksbergs Vaverio.)

153. "The Tournament" by Marjatta Metsovaara of Finland. Strips of thin, flexible copperplate are interlaced with rattan warp and a weft of copper thread. The surface reflects light, and yet the negative space between the copper strips gives the piece an illusion of depth.

154. "Surnia" by Marjatta Metsovaara of Finland. This is a loosely woven textile made up of sisal and plastic yarn mixed with copper thread. The copper thread reflects light on an otherwise transparent surface.

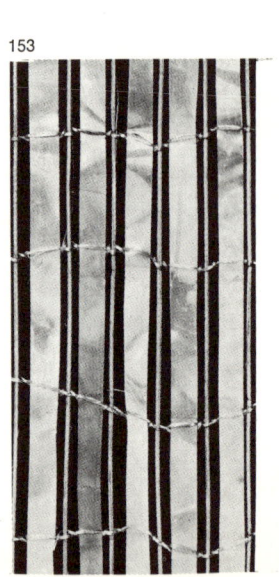

155. "Malin" by Age Faith-Ell of Sweden. This textile was woven in cotton and linen and can be used as curtain material. (Courtesy of AB Kinnasand.)

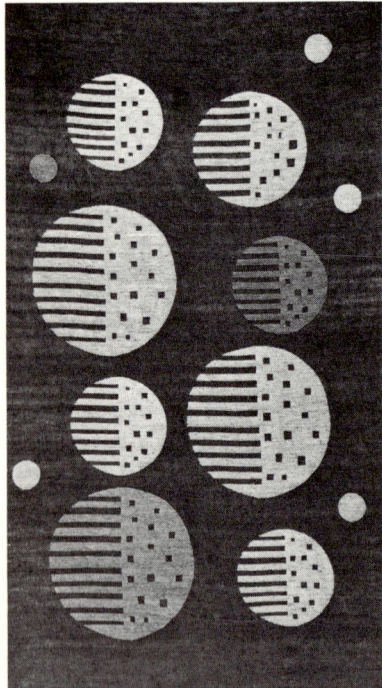

156. Transparency in linen by Maija Kolsi-Makela of Finland. (Courtesy of Helmi Vuorelma.)

157. "Ribbon" by Age Faith-Ell of Sweden. This transparent weave of thick cotton and linen is also intended as curtain material.

158. Detail of transparent linen by Maija Kolsi-Makela of Finland.

159. Linen transparency in tones of blue by Maija Kolsi-Makela of Finland. (Courtesy of Helmi Vuorelma.)

160. Detail of transparency in linen by Maija Kolsi-Makela of Finland. It is so loosely woven that the textile is practically transparent. (Courtesy of Helmi Vuorelma.)

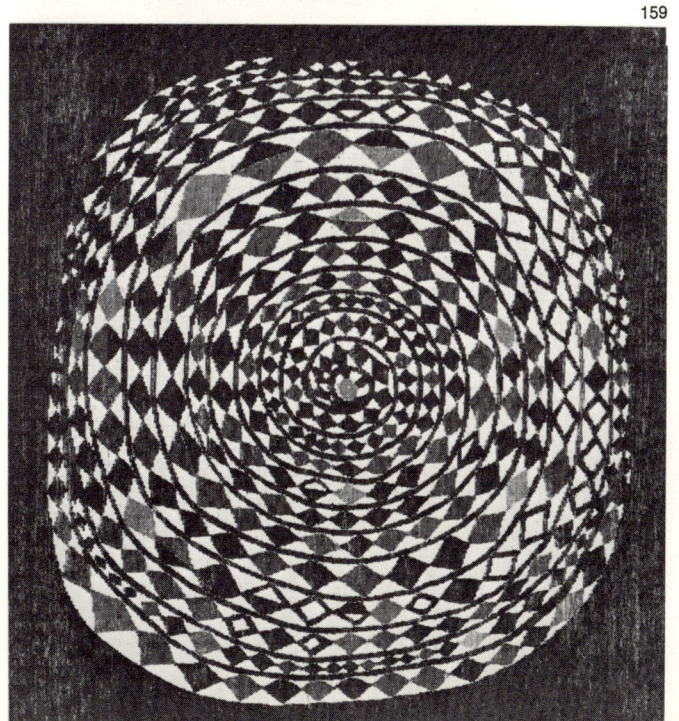

161. Detail of linen transparency by Maija Kolsi-Makela of Finland.

162. "Daalia," transparent weave in linen by Maija Kolsi-Makela of Finland. (Courtesy of Helmi Vuorelma.)

163. Loose, transparent wall hanging by Franka Rasmussen of Denmark. The warp is twisted linen, and the weft is comprised of linen, synthetic yarn, and cotton.

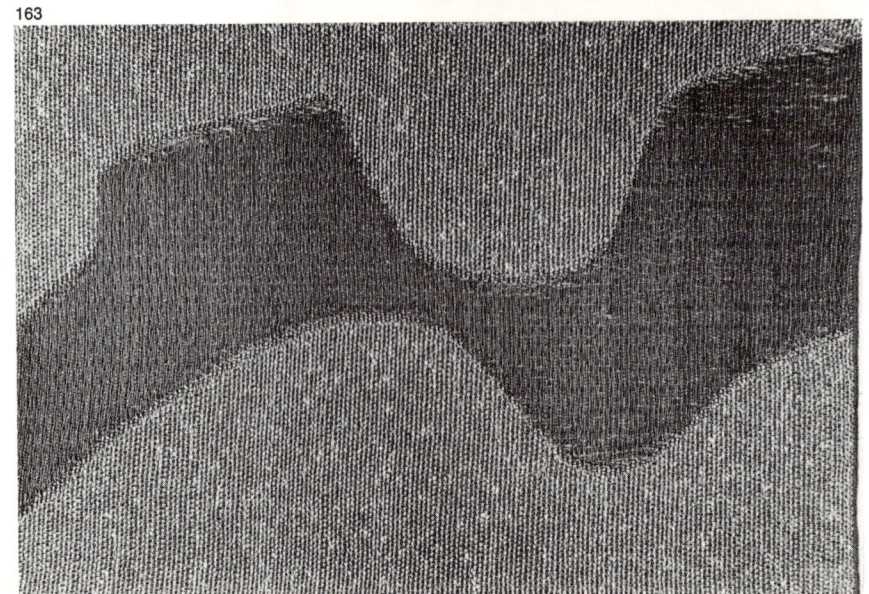

164. Detail of wall hanging by Franka Rasmussen of Denmark. The white form on top combines wool and linen in plain weave; the solid black bands are wool and were woven separately; and the lower forms are made up of linen warp, twisted and left loose, and wool and jute in a plain weave.

165. Detail of transparency by Franka Rasmussen of Denmark. The off-white form combines synthetic yarn in a plain weave and cotton woven in a type of basket-weave braid. The white-formed weft is a variation in linen of the rya knot.

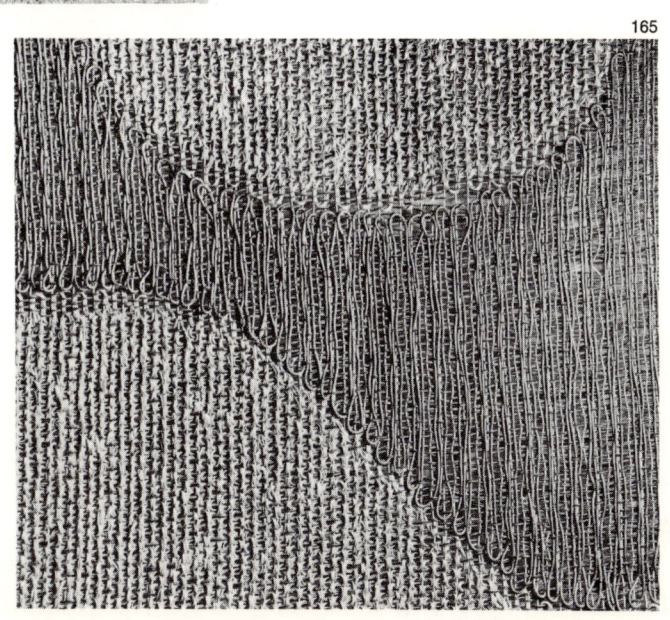

166. Detail of transparent wall hanging by Bodil Bodtker-Naess of Denmark. The technique is the soumak knot with fish line, jute, and linen.

167. "School of Fish," transparent room divider by Bodil Bodtker-Naess of Denmark. This piece was woven on a loom with nylon fish line, linen, flat plastic, and jute marine rope.

168. "School of Fish" (detail) by Bodil Bodtker-Naess of Denmark. Colors include blues, olive, brown, and turquoise.

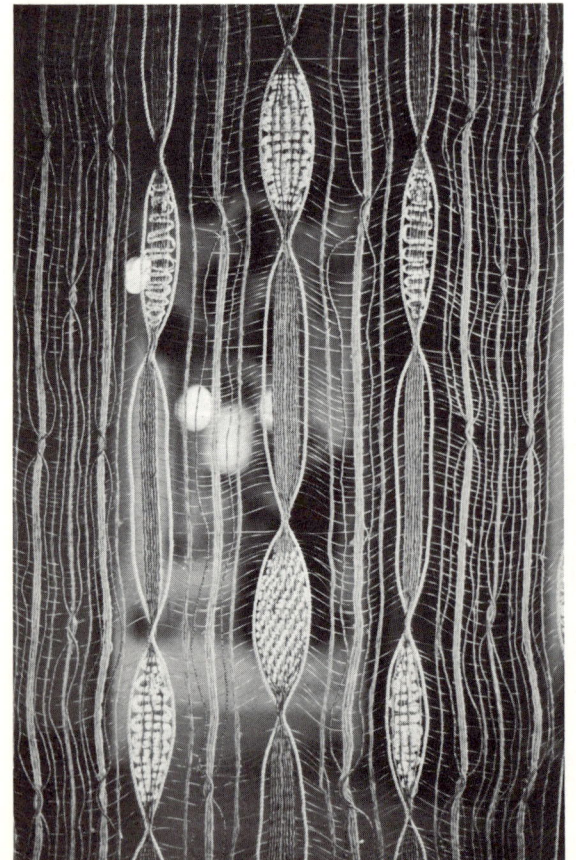

169. "Fool Strips," room divider by Lea Tennberg of Finland. The divider is over 4 feet wide, but was woven on a 3-foot-wide loom by bunching, or puckering the cotton braid in loops. The warp and weft are made up of alternate threads of bleached and unbleached hand-spun linen.

170. "Fool Strips" (detail) by Lea Tennberg of Finland. The linen warp was braided and knotted as it was finished off.

171. Wall hanging in bleached, unbleached, and dyed hand-spun linen by Lea Tennberg of Finland. To retain tension, the piece is stretched on a pine frame.

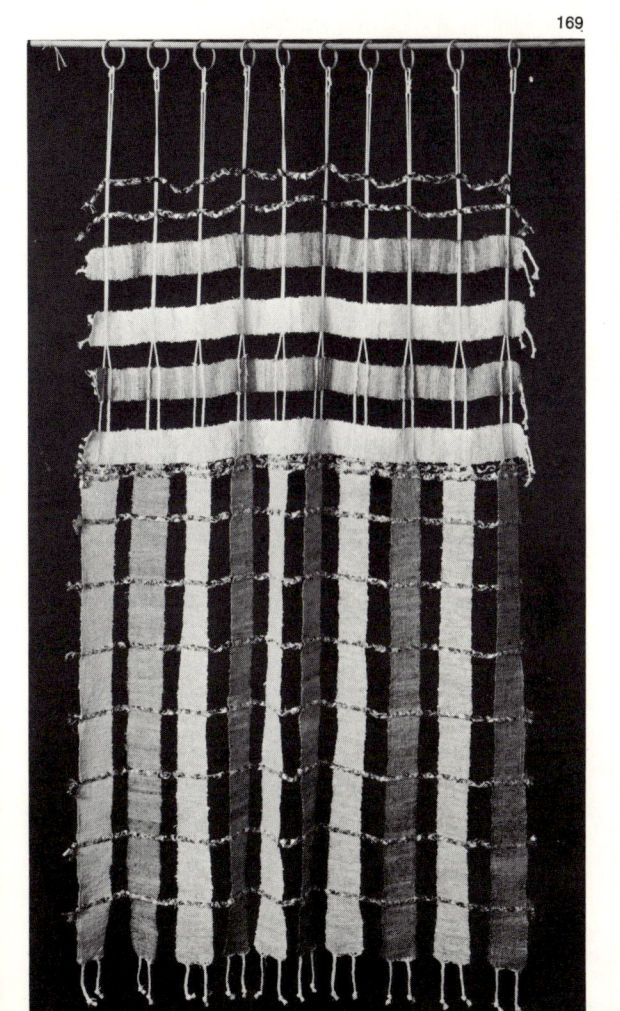

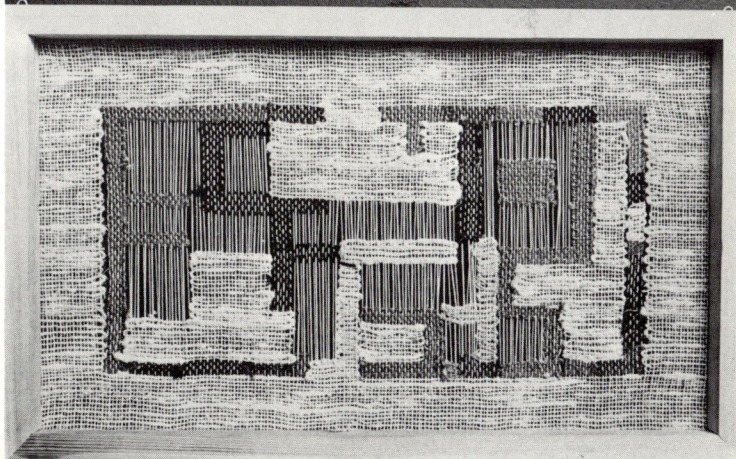

172. Transparent linen by Lis Ahlmann of Denmark. Varying grades of soft linen floss were used in warp and weft. (Courtesy of Den Permanente.)

173. "Mask" by Helle Kaastrup-Olsen of Denmark. This hanging is made from tow yarn and tar bast, with chunks of natural wool set in at the top. (Courtesy of the Danish Society of Arts, Crafts, and Industrial Design.)

174. Binding hand-spun linen threads to develop pattern and transparency. (Courtesy of Lea Tennberg of Finland.)

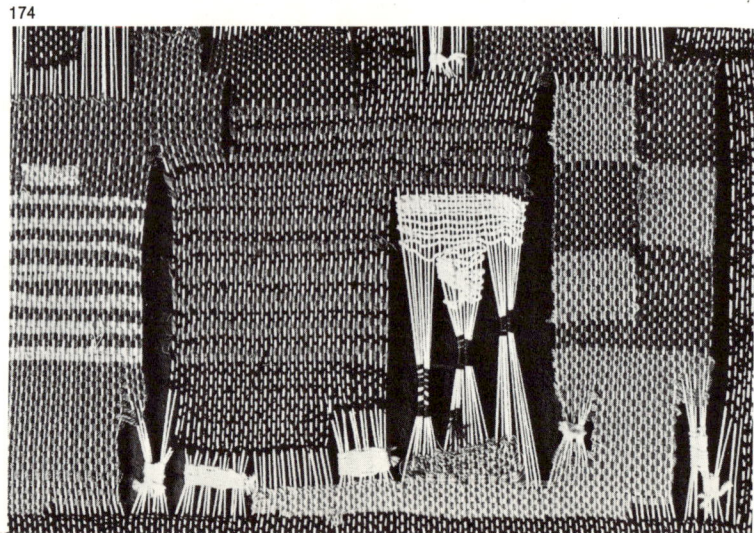

175. Woven wall hanging with transparent application, by Mette Dideriksen of Denmark. Another way of developing transparency is to apply fabric over a woven surface, in this case a transparent fabric over woven sisal and wool. (Courtesy of the Danish Handicraft Guild.)

176. Detail of wall hanging using tar yarn as both warp and weft. By Helle Kaastrup-Olsen of Denmark. (Courtesy of the Danish Handicraft Guild.)

177. Transparent room divider by Oili Maki of Finland. Made from loosely woven wool with beads strung only on the weft.

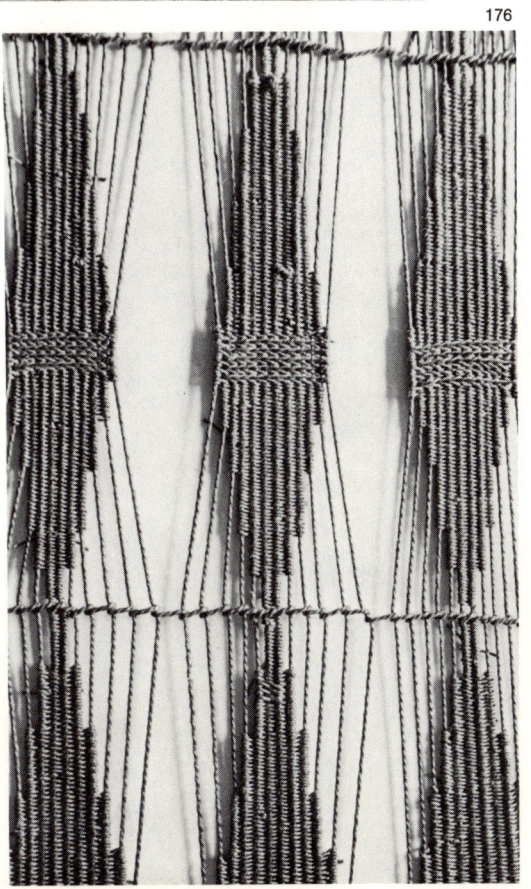

178. Wall hanging by Anne Brodersen of Denmark. It was woven on a loom with a warp of black nylon and a weft of linen, mohair, and string.

179. Transparent wall hanging woven in two layers with linen, tow, and wool measures 78 by 118 centimeters. By Jette Nevers of Denmark. (Courtesy of the Danish Society of Arts, Crafts, and Industrial Design.)

180. "Ship," transparent wall hanging by Nana Nissen of Denmark. (Courtesy of Den Permanente.)

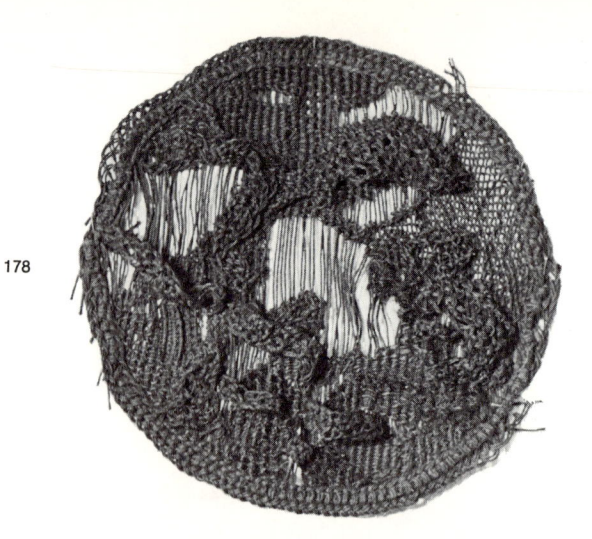

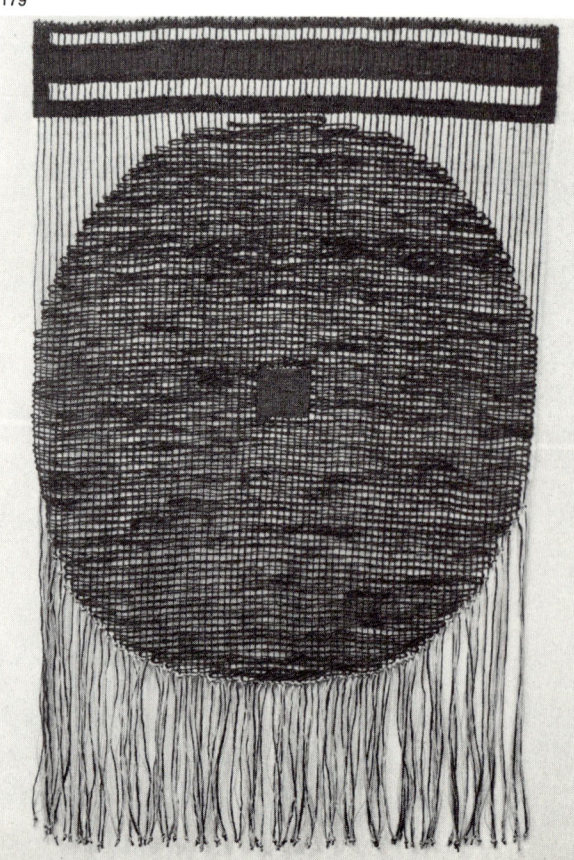

181. Dress made from hemp string looped and spliced around brass rings. By Nana Riisager of Denmark.

182. "Rain Forest," transparency with linen and metal threads, by Viena Mertsalmi of Finland. (Courtesy of the Finnish Design Center.)

183. Wall hanging by Anne Brodersen of Denmark. Woven on a loom using a warp of black nylon and a weft of linen, mohair, and string.

184. Experiment in sisal and polyester with aluminum paint. By Kari Jorgensen of Norway.

185. Detail of technique used to make ring dress. By Nana Riisager of Denmark.

186. Experiment in sisal and polyester (detail) by Kari Jorgensen of Norway.

# FUNCTIONAL WEAVING

187. Woven antie in linen by Birgit Rastrup-Larsen of Denmark. The weaver explains that this is a neckpiece for the man who is tired of standard neckties. The form was woven on a square frame, using a needle in place of a shuttle.

188. Feather poncho by Birgit Rastrup-Larsen of Denmark. This poncho was woven on a loom and then appliquéd with colored feathers. It is an excellent example of how the weaver's contemporary imagery in wall hangings can be carried over into fashion.

189. Wool with sheepskin frame. By Aini Suomi of Finland.

190. Piece in Figure 189 used as a soft, insulated bed cover. The woven front is sewn to a sheepskin back. It can be used as shown or as a wall hanging with the sheepskin as a natural frame. This same technique can be applied equally in making ponchos and capes.

189

190

124

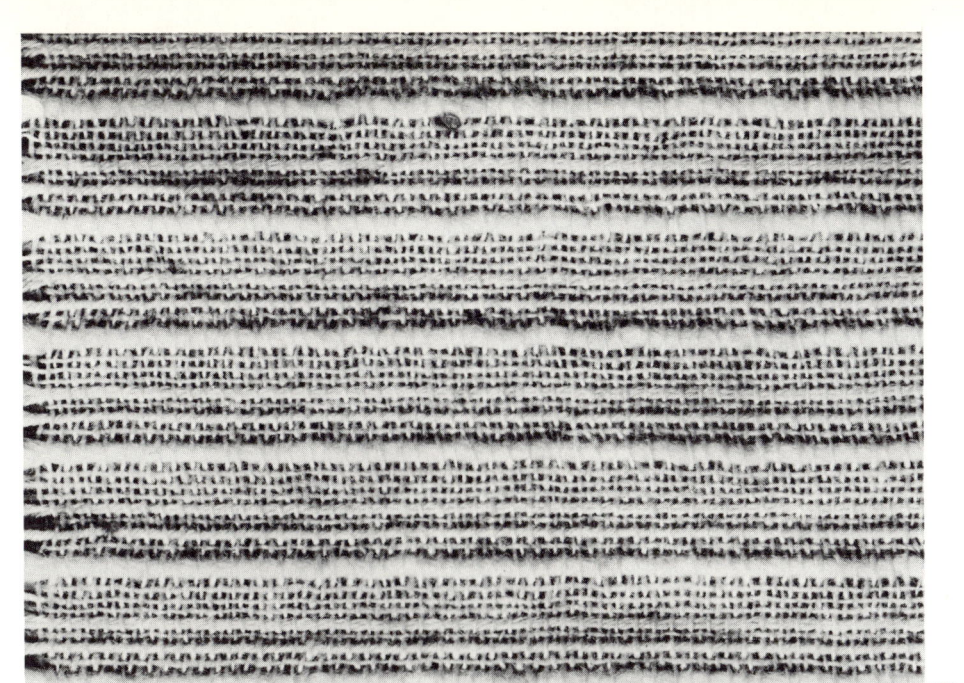

191. "The Weeping Willow" by Marjatta Metsovaara of Finland. This fabric is all wool and was designed for garments.

192. Blanket woven in wool and mohair. By Marjatta Metsovaara of Finland.

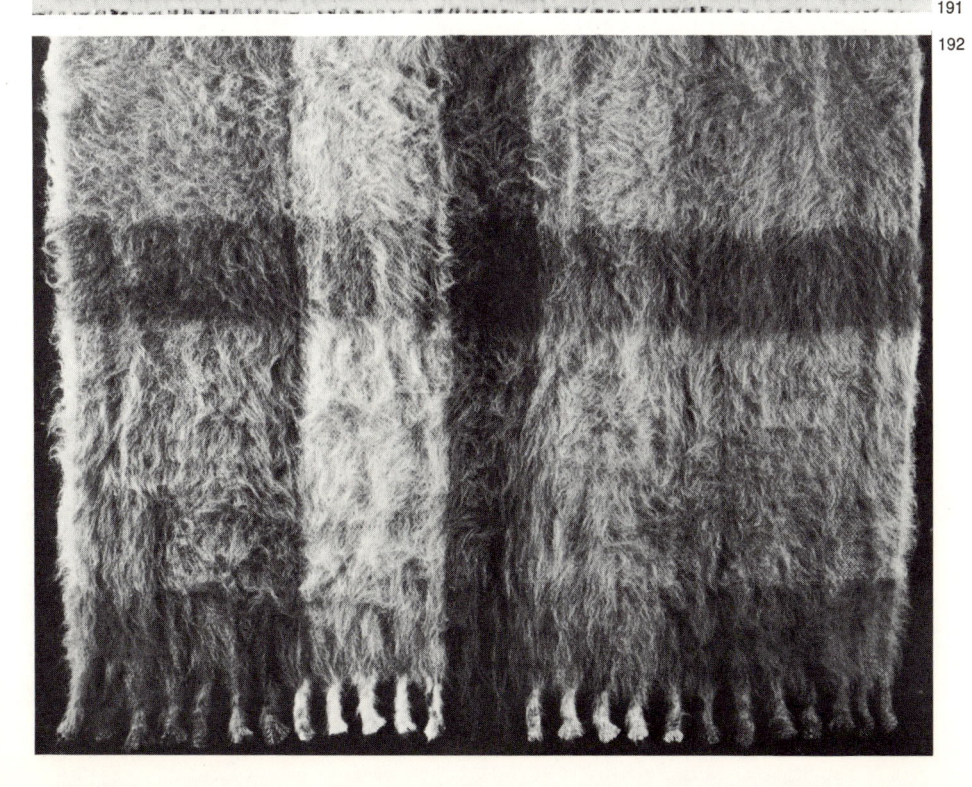

# ACKNOWLEDGMENTS

In addition to the many weavers who contributed to this book, I would like to thank the following organizations and individuals who made my research in Scandinavia possible: Maire Walden and Finnish Press Bureau; Erkki Savolainen and *Look at Finland* magazine; Sinikka Salokorpi and *Avotakka* magazine; the Finnish Design Center and Reino Routamo; the Finnish Society of Crafts and Design and H. O. Gummerus; Ornamo; the National Museum of Finland; and Eila Nevenranta, Kaj Franck, Howard Smith, Matti Timola, and Catharina Kajander—all of Finland. Norsk Design Centrum, Alf Bøe, and Janicke Meyer; *Bonytt* magazine; Landsforbundet Norsk Brukskunst; Dr. and Mrs. Peter Anker; and Siri Blackstad—all of Norway. Svenska Slojdforeningen and Birgitta Willen; the Swedish Institute; Anna-Greta Erkner Annerfalk and Kollegiet for Sverige—Information; Claes-Hokan Wihl, his wife, and the staff at Monsanto Scandinavia Ab; *Sweden Now* magazine; Pal-Nils Nilsson; Hemslojdforbundet for Sverige; Konstindustriskolan, Goteborg, and Marta Rinde-Ramsback; Nordiska Museet, Stockholm; Historiska Museet, Stockholm; *Forum* magazine; and the Form Design Center in Malmo—all of Sweden. The Danish Society of Arts, Crafts, and Industrial Design and Aksel Dahl; the Danish Handicraft Guild, Gertie Wandel, and Hanne Zahle; Den Permanente and Mrs. Ole Wanscher; the Royal Danish Ministry of Foreign Affairs Press Office; *Mobilia* magazine; the Danish Handicraft School; and Ove Hector Nielsen, John Allpass, Helle Olsen, and Mr. and Mrs. Kaj Larsen—all of Denmark.

For travel arrangements, I would like to thank: the Finnish Travel Association and Mrs. Bengt Pihlstrom; Finnair; Oy Finnlines Ab; the Finnish Steamship Company; Bore Lines Ab; the Foreign Ministry of Norway; the Norwegian State Railway; Scandinavian Airlines System; the Swedish State Railway; Swedish American Line; the Danish State Railway; the Royal Danish Ministry of Foreign Affairs; and the United Steamship Company of Denmark.

I would like to thank the following photographers and agencies who have work included in this volume: Otso Pietinen; Eino Makinen; Matti Saanio; Kuvakiila; Foto Jatta; J. Pohjakallio; Foto Pinx; V. Lokuvaamo; P-F Studio; Kirsti Lahtinen; M-L Kartasekowa; Ilmari Kostiainen; Esko Silvanto; Nousiainen; and Hede Foto—all of Finland. Lone Formbid and Guri Tveitt of Norway. Rolf Lind; Herlin & Hoim; K-G Kristofersson; Jeremy Taylor; Dagens Bild; Pal-Nils Nilsson/Tio; Sten D. Dellander/Tio; Atelje Wahlberg; and Marta Rinde-Ramsback—all of Sweden. Simon Plum; Ove Hector Nielsen; Ole Borch Jacobsen; Preben Hultgren; Ole Woldbye; Gregers Nielsen; Carl Rasmussen; Thomas Pedersen; Roald Pay/Delta; Nils Elswing; Lilian Bolvinkel; Viggo Kragmann; and Erik Hansen—all of Denmark.

# MATERIALS FOR FURTHER STUDY

**The following books and periodicals may be ordered directly from their publishers in Europe and the United States:**

*Designed in Finland* (annual), Finnish Foreign Trade Association, Et Esplanadikatu 18, Helsinki 13, Finland.
*Finnish Designers of Today,* Werner Soderstrom Osakeyhtio, Porvoo, Finland (1954).
Kaukonen, Toini-Inkeri, *Finnish Historical Woven Belts,* Suomalaisen Kirjallisuuden Seura, Forssa, Finland (1965).
*Kotiteollisuus* (periodical on handicrafts), Kotiteollisuuden Keskusliitto, Temppelikatu 15-A, Helsinki, Finland.
*Omin Kasin* (periodical on weaving and embroidery), Hietalahdenranta 13, Helsinki 19, Finland.
Perheentupa, Ester, *Kutokaa Itse Kankaanne,* W.S.O.Y. Publishing Co., Porvoo, Finland (1951).
Puromiehen, K. F., *Suomen Museo LVIII* (on ikat dyeing), Kirjapaino Oy., Helsinki (1951).
Pyysalo, Helvi, *Kankaiden Sidokset* (on takana), Otava Publishing Co., Uudenmaankatu 8-12, Helsinki, Finland (1967).
Sirelius, U. T., *The Ryijy Rugs of Finland,* Otava Publishing Co., Uudenmaankatu 8-12, Helsinki, Finland (1926).
Troupp, Lotte, *Modern Finnish Textile,* Otava Publishing Co., Uudenmaankatu 8-12, Helsinki, Finland (1962).

*Bonytt* (periodical), Bygdoy Alle 9, Oslo 2, Norway.

*Norsk Husflid* (periodical), Ø Slottsgate 8, Oslo 1, Norway.
*Norsk Kunsthandverk* (on design), Bonytt Publishing Co., Bygdoy Alle 9, Oslo 2, Norway (1968).

Block, Mary, *Den Stora Vavboken* (on weaving), Bokforlaget Natur Och Kultur, Stockholm, Sweden (1939).
Cyrus, Ulla, *Handbok I Vavning* (on weaving), Lantbruksforbundets Tidskrifts Aktiebolag, Stockholm, Sweden (1950).
Eskerod, Albert, *Swedish Folk Art,* Nordiska Museet, Stockholm, Sweden (1964).
Ingers, Gertrud, *Flamskvavnad,* Ica-Forlaget, Vasteras, Sweden (1961).
*Forum* (periodical), Box 7047, Stockholm 7, Sweden.
*Handicraft in Sweden,* Svenska Hemslojdsforeningarnas Riksforbund, Sturegatan 29, 11129 Stockholm, Sweden.
*Hemslojden* (periodical), Brannkyrkagatan 117, Stockholm, Sweden.
Ingers Gertrud, and Becker, John, *Damast,* Ica-Forlaget, Vasteras, Sweden (1955).
Lunback, Maja, *VI Vaver Till Hemmet* (on weaving), Ica-Forlaget, Vasteras, Sweden (1954).
Lundback, Maja, and Rinde-Ramsback, Marta, *Smavavar* (on weaving), Ica-Forlaget, Vasteras, Sweden.
Lundgren, Tyra, *Marta Maas-Fjetterstrom Och Vav Verkstaden i Bastad* (on weaving), Albert Bonniers Forlag, Stockholm, Sweden (1968).
Manker, Ernst, *People of Eight Seasons,* Cogner and Co., Goteborg, Sweden.

Nylen, Anna-Maja, *Swedish Peasant Costumes,* Nordiska Museet, Stockholm, Sweden (1949).
Segerstad, Ulf Hard af, *Modern Swedish Textiles,* Nordisk Rotogravyr, Stockholm, Sweden (1963).
Stavenow, Ake, and Huldt, Ake H., *Svensk Form,* Gothia Publishing, Stockholm, Sweden (1964).
Wager, Kerstin and Ulla, *Rag Weavings,* Nordiska Museet, Stockholm, Sweden (1967).

*Dansk Husflidstidende,* Danish Society for Handicraft, Kong Gerogsvej 70, Copenhagen F, Denmark.
*Dansk Kunsthaandvaerk* (journal), Danish Society of Arts, Crafts, and Industrial Design, Bredgade 58, 1260 Copenhagen K, Denmark.
Enovoldsen, Christian og Birgit, *Brugskunst, Møbler, Textiler, Lamper,* Arkitektens Forlag, Nyhavn 43, Copenhagen K, Denmark (1958).
*Haandarbejdets Fremme* (periodical), Danish Handicraft Guild, Vimmelskaftet 38, Copenhagen K, Denmark.
*Mobilia,* Snekkersten, Denmark.
Møller, Svend Erik, *34 Scandinavian Designers,* Mobilia Publishers, Snekkersten, Denmark (1967).
Salicath, Bent, and Karlsen, Arne, *Modern Danish Textiles,* Arkitektens Forlag, Nyhavn 43, Copenhagen K, Denmark (1961).
*Scandinavian Times Magazine,* Kompagnistraede 39, 1209 Copenhagen K, Denmark.

*A Treasury of Scandinavian Design,* Hassings Forlag AS, Vodroffsvej 26, Copenhagen, Denmark (1961).

*The American Scandinavian Review,* American Scandinavian Foundation, 127 E. 73 St., New York, N.Y. 10021.
Cohn, F. S., *Swedish-English Textile Glossary for Weavers,* Berkeley Publishing (1944).
Cyrus, Ulla, *Manual of Swedish Handweaving,* Charles T. Brandford, Boston, Mass.
*Fisherman's Knots and Nets,* Cornell Maritime Press, Cambridge, Md. 21613.

*Handbook of Knots,* Cornell Maritime Press, Cambridge, Md. 21613.
*Leather Braiding,* Cornell Maritime Press, Cambridge, Md. 21613.
Plath, Iona, *The Decorative Arts of Sweden,* Charles Scribner's Sons, New York (1948).
*Square Knot Handicraft Guide,* Cornell Maritime Press, Cambridge, Md. 21613.

Hall, Wendy, *The Finns and Their Country,* Mac Parrish & Co., Ltd., 2 Portman Street, London W1, England (1967).
Saarts, Martha, *Finnish Textiles,* F. Lewis Publishers, Leigh-On-Sea, England (1954).
Segerstad, Ulf Hard af, *Scandinavian Design,* Studio Books, London, England (1961).

**Weaving supplies are available in Scandinavia from the following mail-order firms:**

**Yarn and weaving supplies**

The Friends of Finnish Handicrafts,
Yrjonkatu 13, Helsinki, Finland (rya sets)
Helmi Vuorelma Oy, Lahti, Finland
(cotton, linen, and wool)
Helsingin Villakehraamo Oy,
Helsinki, Finland (Draylon)
Helsingin Villakehraamo Oy,
Vattuniemenkatu 20, Helsinki, Finland
(Draylon rya sets)
Kotivilla Oy, Jarvela, Finland
Monsanto Scandinavia Ab, Eriksgatan
32-B, Helsinki, Finland (acrylon yarns)
Neovius Oy, Munkkisaarenkatu 2,
Helsinki 15, Finland (rya sets)
Tampella Linen Mill, Tampere, Finland
(linen)
Vokki Oy, Vainamoisenkatu 31-B,
Helsinki 10, Finland

The Norwegian Home Arts and Crafts
Association (Husfliden), Mollergate 4,
Oslo, Norway

Aktiebolaget Nordiska Kompaniet,
Box 7159, Stockholm 7, Sweden
Hemslojdforbundet for Sverige,
Sturegatan 29, Stockholm, Sweden

CUM, Rømersgade 5, Copenhagen K,
Denmark
The Danish Handicraft Guild,
Vimmelskaftet 38, Copenhagen K,
Denmark
Julius Koch, Norrebrogade 52,
Copenhagen, Denmark
Tomtex, Tordenskjoldsgade 23, 1055,
Copenhagen K, Denmark

**Damask looms**
Varpapuu Oy, Pieksamaki, Finland

**Weaving stools, spinning wheels, etc.**
The Finnish Design Center,
Kasarmikatu 19, Helsinki 13, Finland

Oy Stockmann Ab, Aleksanterinkatu 52,
Helsinki 10, Finland

**Wood beads for finishing warp ends**
Aarikka, Nokiantie 2, Helsinki, Finland
Oy Stockmann Ab, Aleksanterinkatu 52,
Helsinki 10, Finland
For additional information on Finnish
suppliers write to: Reino Routamo,
director, the Finnish Design Center,
Kasarmikatu 19, Helsinki 13, Finland.

**The following Scandinavian schools offer courses in weaving:**

Ateneum, Railway Square,
Helsinki 10, Finland
Fredrika Wetterhoffin
Kotiteollisuusopettajaopisto,
Hameenlinna, Finland (for teachers)

Statens Handverks og
Kunstindustriskole, Ullevalsvejen 5,
Oslo 1, Norway
Statens Kunstindustriskole, Bergen,
Norway
Statens Laererskole i Forming,
Cort Adelersgt. 33, Oslo, Norway
Konstfackskolan, Valhallavegen 191,
Stockholm, Sweden
Konstindustriskolan, Kristinelundsgatan
6-8, Goteborg C, Sweden
Textilinstitutet, Boras, Sweden

The Danish Handicraft Guild School,
Bredgade 77, Copenhagen K, Denmark

**Scandinavian design and handicraft societies and exhibitions:**

The Finnish Design Center,
Kasarminkatu 19, Helsinki, Finland
The Finnish Society of Crafts and
Design, Unionkatu 30, Helsinki 10,
Finland
Ornamo, Ainonkatu 3, Helsinki 10,
Finland

Norsk Design Centrum, Drammensvejen
40, Oslo 2, Norway
Landsforbundet Norsk Brukskunst,
Uranienborgvejen 2, Oslo 1, Norway

The National Association of Swedish
Handicraft Societies, Mimervagen 8,
Djursholm 2, Sweden
Svenska Slojdforeningen, Nybrogatan 7,
Box 7047, Stockholm 7, Sweden

The Danish Handicraft Guild,
Vimmelskaftet 38, Copenhagen K,
Denmark
The Danish Society of Arts, Crafts, and
Industrial Design, Bredgade 58,
1260 Copenhagen K, Denmark
Den Permanente, Vesterport,
Copenhagen V, Denmark

The Society for the Promotion of
Lappish Culture, Kunmeltie 11 C 31,
Tapiola, Finland

## DATE DUE

| DE 14 '90 | | | |
|---|---|---|---|
| | | | |

52523

746.1
W697